BELOVEDNESS

Finding God (and Self) on Campus

D1566186

edited by
JAMES FRANKLIN & BECKY ZARTMAN

CHURCH
PUBLISHING
INCORPORATED

Church Publishing
19 East 34th Street
New York, NY 10016
www.churchpublishing.org

Cover design by Marc Whitaker, MTWdesign
Interior design and typesetting by Beth Oberholtzer

Library of Congress Cataloging-in-Publication Data

Names: Franklin, James, editor. | Zartman, Becky, editor.
Title: Belovedness : finding God (and self) on campus / edited by James Franklin, and
    Becky Zartman.
Identifiers: LCCN 2019057521 (print) | LCCN 2019057522 (ebook) |
    ISBN 9781640652835 (paperback) | ISBN 9781640652842 (epub)
Subjects: LCSH: College students--Religious life. | College students--Conduct of life. |
    Universities and colleges--Religion. | Spiritual life.
Classification: LCC BV639.C6 B45 2020 (print) | LCC BV639.C6 (ebook) |
    DDC 248.8/34--dc23
LC record available at https://lccn.loc.gov/2019057521
LC ebook record available at https://lccn.loc.gov/2019057522

For all our students,
who taught us how
to be in ministry
on campus.

CONTENTS

AN INVITATION TO BELOVEDNESS

What we wish for you, more than anything else, is for you to know how beloved you are.

We know this concept of belovedness sounds woo-woo, like we're going to break out some crystals and set some good intentions. We know belovedness can seem schmaltzy, like some kind of Precious Moments Sunday school cop-out, or just plain naive, as if we live in some kind of self-help fantasy world where accepting yourself and loving yourself fixes everything. We know what "belovedness" evokes. But that feel-good vibe is not what we're talking about here. Belovedness is far more existential, and matters far, far more than how you feel about yourself on any given day.

What we call belovedness, which is understanding your true worth as a child of God, is freedom. Freedom to become fully yourself, surely, but also freedom to become wholly God's. Saints, the heroes of our faith, and sometimes heroes of the world, are nothing other than people who have figured out their own belovedness and have been set free. The saints have discovered what the Apostle Paul figured out, writing back in the first century: "For I am convinced that neither death, nor life, nor angels, nor rulers, nor things present, nor things to come, nor powers, nor height, nor depth, nor anything else in all creation, will be able to separate us from the love of God in Christ Jesus our Lord" (Rom. 8:38–39). The saints know, deep within themselves, that the love of God is all that matters, and then they just go for it.

And when they do, the world changes.

Desmond Tutu helped to end apartheid peacefully in South Africa. In America, Fred Rogers changed hundreds of thousands of children's lives. Dorothy Day started a movement of mercy. Oscar Romero spoke against torture and social injustice. Evelyn Underhill helped stodgy Brits engage with their spirituality, even in the midst of war. Dietrich Bonhoeffer fought Nazis and bore witness to the Beloved Community. In Frances Perkins's quest for labor rights, she became the first woman appointed to the US Cabinet, passing laws against child labor and starting Social Security. And that's just this century. Martyrs, apostles, prophets, preachers, teachers, monastics, mystics, social reformers, doctors, scientists, writers, environmentalists, public servants, historians, scholars, composers, artists, architects, philanthropists, abolitionists, liberators—there are as many ways to be a saint as there are people in the world. What made them saints was their fidelity to who they are and whose they are. The love of God set them free and enabled them to change the world.

These are just the saints whose stories we tell. But there are millions of nameless saints who have come before us, going back to the earliest days of the church and right up until our present day. These saints have been set free by their faith in God to show miraculous amounts of love and to do what is right. From those who fearlessly nursed the plague victims of ancient Rome to the LGBTQ+ community during the AIDS crisis of the 80s and 90s, from those who have smuggled slaves to freedom to those who pluck refugees from the sea today, there have been Christians who have risked everything to love their neighbor, because they have known God's love. Of course, the church and its members have also often done an incredible amount of harm as well. What the life-giving work has in common is love that knows no bounds. What the toxic colonialism and violence has in common is the inability to see that God created and loves all people. Here's the takeaway: how we understand God's love for ourselves and others matters. A lot.

Knowing you are loved sets you free to be yourself and then to use the whole of yourself to participate in God's endeavor in the world. The good news is that you don't have to be a saint of towering compassion like Mother Theresa or a saint of towering genius like Karl Barth. Rather, to be a saint, you just have to be yourself. God made you to be you, because God needs you for who you are, where you are. Even, and maybe especially, when you're going to college. College is a time for making decisions about who you want to be in the world and how you want to live in the world. This is the time and place where you get to choose. Are you going to choose to live into your belovedness and change the world?

About This Book

This book is an exploration of that question, although perhaps it's easier to first outline what this book is not. This book is not a handbook for how to successfully navigate college, although we hope you do so. This book is not a rulebook that will tell you whether you're doing college correctly or not. This is not a book about "what the Bible says," although we do wrestle with scripture. This book is not a book of sage advice from college chaplains, although generally, chaplains do give great advice. Instead, this book asks a single question that gets refracted through different topics: How would you [fill in the blank] if you knew you were loved beyond all measure? How are you going to choose to live into your belovedness?

We've asked some of our wisest and best chaplain colleagues from a variety of denominational backgrounds to ask that question, as well as help you ask that question for yourself. How would you make choices about your life if you knew you were loved beyond all measure? How would you approach success and failure, your relationships, or prayer? How would you approach being LGBTQ+? Or sex? Or partying? Mental health? How would you navigate life's difficulties if you truly knew how much you were loved? The first chapter explores belovedness, and then the following chapters ask these questions from the perspective of owning your own belovedness while in college. Our hope is that as you read you'll ask these questions for yourself, because the only person who can truly answer the questions we place before you is you.

We also firmly believe that these questions are best asked and answered in community. When we ask these questions in community, we provide each other the love and support that it takes to answer honestly, and by so doing, become who we are. We hope that this book will be used by youth groups getting ready to send their seniors to college and by college chaplains with first-year college students (or at any point during college). However, we realize that not everyone has access to chaplains, so we've provided a DIY small group guide in the back. Anyone who is willing to help guide a conversation can lead a small group in rich and life-giving conversation. No degree required.

Of course, you can also read the book on your own, but we hope you'll talk about these questions with your friends and adults you trust. Starting in college and moving into young adulthood, how you choose to answer these questions can and will shape the rest of your life. What's tricky about these questions is that if you don't thoughtfully ask them now, life will, whether you've thought about them or not. For instance, you will have to deal with the experience of failure at some point, regardless of whether you've thought about it or not. We hope that by taking the time to reflect faithfully on these questions, you'll be better prepared to answer the questions that life throws at you when the time comes, and to better own your belovedness.

We also hope you'll read sections of the book that may not directly apply to you, like the chapter about being LGBTQ+ or dealing with mental illness. Part of recognizing your own belovedness is recognizing the belovedness of others. We invite you into the questions that may not have direct bearing on your life right now, but probably will for you or the people you love in the future.

Whether you are in college or on your way to college, buckle up. What you choose matters, and who you choose to be, matters. It's about to get real.

CHAPTER 1

BELOVEDNESS

James Franklin

God looked over everything [God] had made;
it was so good, so very good! (Genesis 1:31, The Message)

I found myself in the belly of a steel beast. The summer before my junior year, I was sent to the Persian Gulf, where my home was a military transport ship for two months. I was in Navy ROTC and had planned on becoming a helicopter pilot for the Marines. While aboard, a few ROTC students and I had to share bunking space with a platoon of these elite soldiers. The Marines were awaiting the next mission and in that liminal space, they rested, called home to loved ones, exercised incessantly, or played video games until 4:00 a.m. Every. Single. Night. And it was here, in the midst of a crowded berth of hardened scout snipers and Halo, I heard the still small voice calling me "Beloved."

I should say, in the belly of the beast is where I found myself. Or more accurately, I was awakened to my own belovedness. You see, just a few months prior, my father died suddenly of a heart attack and I was in the midst of a spiraling depression like never before. I was lonely and grieving. I was angry with God. I was angry with the military for sending me so far away from the people I needed most—my family. What were they thinking? "Here's an angry, lonely, depressed, and confused kid: let's send him halfway around the world amongst bombs and live ammunition!" I felt a million miles away.

The all-night Halo matches proved to be a welcome distraction from all the grief and loneliness. Sleep meant dreams about my dad and lots of crying (which was an odd thing to do around military folk who are told to "lock it up!"). But it turned out I had more in common with those Marines than I thought. They themselves were dealing with trauma, grieving the loss of friends or spouses who had left them during deployment. They too were running from all the pain because they had to keep their focus.

One night after a few rounds of Halo with my leather-neck bunkmates, I crawled into my third-story bed. With adrenaline still pumping and general insomnia, I read *Blue Like Jazz*, a memoir by Donald Miller about his college experience and reconciling how a God could be a loving father while his own father had abandoned him.

In the midst of all this, I suddenly had an experience of knowing, from deep within me, that I was beloved. Somehow it made sense that even though my father was gone, his love for me remained. I came to realize that even though it was hard to see God or feel loved by someone who I couldn't see, I was the object of that *agapē* love. I experienced it. I felt it. I knew it.

Some have a dramatic conversion experience. But I wouldn't call my experience dramatic or even a conversion—it was closer to an awakening or waking up, for the first time to my true self. It was the moment I remembered and realized that my transformation was happening slowly, over time, and after being told over and over: you are loved, you are loved, you are loved. This was just the first time it sank in.

In *Life of the Beloved*, Henri Nouwen describes the process of belovedness as claiming for ourselves first, then proclaiming. Nouwen wrote to a student: "From the moment we claim the truth of being the Beloved, we are faced with the call to become who we are. Becoming the Beloved is the great spiritual journey we have to make."[1] Claiming our own belovedness is a tough process and one that is in direct opposition to the world around us. But it's different than the simplistic (and false) dichotomies of good versus evil, body and soul, or two opposing teams on a field. It doesn't compete for space in the world. It really is more like an awakening. But what does it mean to awaken to this mystical frontier of your innermost being?

Claiming belovedness means letting go. And letting go hurts. Belovedness asks us to let go and submit to a process that grates and chafes

---

1. Henri J. M. Nouwen, *Life of the Beloved* (New York: Crossroad, 1992), 43.

away at falsehoods, which we've begun to accept as fact, that seek to tell us who we really are. Because the rejection we experience and the constant narrative of unworthiness or how unlovable we are tries to bury our belovedness. The slow awakening to belovedness can be painful as we try to go against the flow of God calling us beloved. Why do we always try to swim upstream when we can flourish in the freedom of floating in a river of grace?

When I first awoke to my belovedness, it hurt. I knew that I was beloved beyond all else and there was nothing anyone could do to change it. But it meant letting go of my ego—that I thought I knew what I wanted to do with my life and the myth that I was in charge of making that life. Yet even in the midst of that agony of letting go, I could feel God holding me in the comfort of my very-goodness, my being made-wholeness, my belovedness.

Another way of speaking about awakening to belovedness is "theophany" (which is just a fancy word for "God showing up" or having an experience of the holy). I can feel and experience belovedness when I'm attuned to that quiet voice that breaks through the cacophony of noise and voices telling me what is important. The harshness of advertisements, pundits, elected officials, and even preachers has divided us and told us to fear the person who doesn't look like us. In college, these voices are multiplied with fears of not living up to parents, school, or our own expectations. Or a voice that seeks perfectionism or is scared to death of failure.

That which keeps us from theophany and belovedness is discordance and fear. Where belovedness unifies and creates belonging, the voices of noise and anxiety divide and drive us to isolation. Fear shouts, "No one will ever love you." Belovedness speaks, "All are precious to God." Fear builds a wall; from behind that wall we start to look like an episode of *Hoarders*, clinging to whatever we can. Belovedness creates free and open space for true friendship and community to happen. Fear is a prison of our own making. Belovedness is freedom. And it is knowing that, in spite of all our shit and brokenness, we are loved and we belong.

Awakening is a homecoming to the garden of your Genesis. There you will find the voice calling you "very good." It rouses a truth that lay dormant deep down. It is a truth I suspect you've known at some level. Although my own awakening is ongoing, it has taken me thirty years to claim "I am beloved" (even though I suspect I'll never comprehend it). It is pure wonder. It is pure gift. It is mysterious.

Belovedness Began in a Garden

I know who you are.

My guess is, you do too.

Our story of belovedness begins at the beginning with a loving God who says, "Let us make humankind in our image" (Gen. 1:26). God created all there is—including humanity—and called it "very good." God, throughout scripture, chases people with the truth of their original design, which was their "very goodness." God's dream was that you would know it and live from within that truth. Another name for this "very goodness" could be "belovedness," which began long ago in a garden. The Garden of Eden was Jewish allegory and beautiful poetry for telling ourselves and others who we are and how we are supposed to be: we are God's beloved children, created in God's own image. As Julian of Norwich said, we are not just simply created by God but *of* God.[2] That's right. You're not only created in God's image but you, at your innermost being, are made divine.

Let that settle within you. Have you always been told just how unlovable you are or how you are lower than worm food? If so, belovedness may sound radical. (It is!) Even if you've grown up in a religious tradition (or none at all) that also begins in love, you might need some time for this truth to wash over you as you begin to claim and experience belovedness for yourself.

Why write about belovedness and why does it matter in college? Belovedness is the answer to a question your heart asks. It's the whisper heard from a "still, small voice" (1 Kings 19:12). It's the original blessing that the Word, the Christ, the Son of God, whispered at creation. In

---

2. Julian of Norwich, *Revelations of Divine Love,* trans. Elizabeth Spearing (Harmondsworth: Penguin, 1998), 129.

college, your hearts ask: "Who am I?" This question is more profound than you may realize, for it is the beginning of your own awakening. In college, while so much is up in the air; while myriad, loud voices tell you who you are and what is important, the small voice whispers, *You are beloved.*

Perhaps it would be better to follow our question of "who am I" with "who am I not?" Often, there is much in the way of beginning to claim or experience belovedness as truth. I'm thinking of the inner voice saying: "No one would love me if they knew the real me." You are not your grades, the number of likes on your social media, the number of friends you have, the shaming you receive; you are not the guilt you hear from the pulpit. Whether you've experienced it explicitly or had it implied, I'm willing to guess you've been told, "You are not [fill in the blank] enough," and "You are not worthy of love." I call b.s. on that.

I'm saying the opposite: you are worthy of love. You are enough. Just as you are. Full stop. Nadia Bolz-Weber, a Lutheran pastor, writer, and theologian says, "You will never become your ideal self. God loves your *actual* self."[3] My brothers, sisters, and nonbinary kin, my straight and LGBTQ+ folks: God did not mess up when God created you. In fact there is nothing wrong with you (as far as how you are made). We all have our issues.

Let's Talk about Sin ... and Belovedness

In my first year of college, my then girlfriend Nicole abruptly asked me one night before we were about to watch *Pirates of the Caribbean*, "Do you believe people are created inherently good . . . or evil?" Raised going to church and as a preacher's kid, I knew the story began in God calling things "good" (and not evil) in Genesis. But I also knew about "the fall" and sin. So after a moment, I replied, "Good? I don't know. Now can we just watch *Pirates*?" She just looked at me and said, "Hmmm." It was a test. I failed. (Needless to say, our relationship didn't last much longer.)

---

3. Nadia Bolz-Weber, round table discussion at Wild Goose Festival, Hot Springs, NC, July 14, 2017.

Being an optimist and a person who was raised hearing about God's love for us, I believed it! But Nicole opened my eyes to the fact that so many of us buy into a narrative that begins outside the Garden, in the wilderness. A narrative that would let us believe that we are first and foremost sinful, depraved, and inherently broken. Nicole brings up a good question: What about sin?

Sin does not define you and it is certainly not the most-true aspect of your being. The most compelling definition of sin I've found is: "The seeking of our own will instead of the will of God, thus distorting our relationship with God, with other people, and with all creation."[4] I love this definition of sin as "distortion" because it's not just something we do or something wrong with us—it's about the lack of something between us and God and our relationships with the people we meet and how we treat mother earth. Sin exists as a lack of love. In this lacking space, we find belovedness hard to accept and walk the other way from it and from Christ's love. The real sin is in treating others and ourselves as though we're not beloved by God. In walking away, we begin to believe that brokenness is the original design and we, as hurt people, hurt people in return.

In her book *Original Blessing: Putting Sin in Its Rightful Place*, Danielle Shroyer writes that God's first language is blessing and not calling out sin: "Original blessing means realizing your sin is not the most important thing about you, even if the world—or the church—makes you feel like it is."[5] Countless Christian traditions have exploited original sin and thrived on fear. Sadly, their voices at times seem louder than the still, small voice of belovedness. It makes sense if you think about it: if you start with sin instead of blessing, you end up with a punitive system where God has to be appeased and the death and resurrection of Jesus means salvation is conditional on how you act. Under this system, you can lose that salvation and you can be cast out of the Garden over and over if you don't act right. Not to mention, under this system, war, vio-

---

4. The Book of Common Prayer, 848.

5. Danielle Shroyer, *Original Blessing: Putting Sin in Its Rightful Place* (Minneapolis, Augsburg Fortress Press, 2016), 24.

lence, and retributive justice are all validated because we're all depraved and only some are "in."

I'm here to say that the narrative of very goodness and belovedness was not broken by sin. We have free will and we can deny our belovedness to the hell we choose. As Jeff, my theologian friend and mentor, says, "We can deny that truth straight to hell. But the truth is still there waiting for us to turn around." But when we begin in blessing and very goodness, we see that our belovedness was there all along and Jesus Christ came to reveal it. In the cross, God's restoration was complete. Our belovedness (which was always there but hard to see) was veiled by death and that distortion of sin. Do you see where I'm going with this? We're not here to call out or name sins. You and I are sick of the voice telling us of all that we are not and all that we will never be because of how we look or where we're from or how we're made. Theologian John Phillip Newell says, "I do not believe that the gospel, which literally means, "Good News" is given to tell us that we have failed or been false. That is not news, and it is not good!"[6] I'm not concerned with who is in and who is out—that's damaging, heretical, and hurtful. Lord knows we've had enough of that voice.

I want to tell you of another voice. Mark begins his gospel with Jesus appearing at a river to be baptized. When he emerges from the water, a voice is heard saying: "You are my Son, the Beloved; with you I am well pleased" (Mark 1:11). Christ is at the center of this belovedness because Jesus is the Beloved. He grounds this truth and community in the cosmic hope that we know the one who is always whispering to us, "You are beloved." The one who is constantly calling us homeward, the one who is unfailingly, unconditionally loving us. The one calling us back to the garden.

When the church was co-opted into empire by Constantine in the fourth century, it moved away from an understanding of Christ as having recapitulated, once and for all, this vision of the very goodness of creation (including you and me) being made beloved once again through the Beloved, Jesus Christ. Instead, it moved toward a notion that you

---

6. John Phillip Newell, *Christ of the Celts* (San Francisco: Jossey-Bass, 2008), 8.

and I are created evil and only the Church (as the gatekeeper to grace and the explainer of scripture) could save you from your sinful nature. This may sound extremely reductionistic of nearly two thousand years of church history. But in fact, it missed the point that Jesus Christ is at the beginning, middle, and end of the story of belovedness. It missed the mark and made knowing God all about religion instead of relationship. How ironic, as God's very nature as Trinity is best described as an eternal dance between Father, Son, and Holy Spirit (Creator, Redeemer, Sustainer) in a relationship of love. Don't hear me wrong: religion and the church try, imperfectly, to model this community of love, forgiveness, and grace to the world—the forces that bind the Trinity and us to one another through Christ. Worship in church is still our ideal community of following Jesus. Jean Vanier, the late-theologian and a lifelong Roman Catholic said:

> Stop wasting time running after the perfect community. Live your life fully in your community today. Stop seeing the flaws—and thank God there are some! Look rather at your own defects and know that you are forgiven and can, in your turn, forgive others and today enter into the conversion of love.[7]

Church still strives to be this loving community modeling the life of Jesus. Christ came to reveal, forgive, and heal—the Gospel of John says: "God did not send the Son into the world to condemn the world, but in order that the world might be saved through him" (3:17). Paul later understood this as Christ dying "for all; therefore all have died . . . and he died for all, so that those who live might live no longer for themselves but for him who died and was raised for them" (2 Cor. 5:14–15). Notice it is in past tense: "Died for all." It is not a conditional death that requires an exchange for our sins—only becoming true if we ask it. We have been spoken for, our lives claimed, and death was defeated once and for all. Paul speaks in past tense not as Christ's incarnation, death, and resurrection as happening just one time but as once that carries on for eternity.

---

7. Jean Vanier, *Community and Growth* (Mahwah: Paulist Press, 1989), 46–47.

Richard Rohr, who might be one of the most important theological voices of our time, writes that if Jesus Christ was limited to one event, namely, the cross, at one point in time, then

> the implications of our very selective seeing have been massively destructive for history and humanity. Creation was deemed profane, a pretty accident, a mere backdrop for the real drama of God's concern—which is always and only us. . . . It is impossible to make individuals feel sacred inside of a profane, empty, or accidental universe.[8]

Instead, seeing that Christ was at the beginning when God said, "very good," means Jesus Christ is in all things—including you. The Gospel of John begins with Genesis language alongside language of Jesus Christ as the "Word"; that is, as the one present at creation and whose being is of God: "In the beginning was the Word and the Word was with God and the Word was God. He was in the beginning with God. All things came into being through him" (John 1:1–3). Rohr writes one of the most beautiful interpretations of the Incarnation: "[I]nstead of saying that God came *into* the world through Jesus, maybe it would be better to say that Jesus came *out of* an already Christ-soaked world."[9] In other words, God was never absent because of the fall in the Garden. We were never separated from God. On the contrary, because Christ, the Beloved, was there at the beginning speaking belovedness into all things, Christ emerges through Jesus to reveal our being, made beloved through him. Again, Paul writes in Colossians 3:11: "There is only Christ. He is everything and he is in everything" (paraphrased).

Just as the sun shines on us and our blocking the light creates shadow, so does denying belovedness create the shadow of sin. However, as Danielle Shroyer puts it, "Blessing allows you to look at the brokenness of the world (and within yourself) with grace and loving-kindness, rather than with shame, hostility, or despair."[10] So when we experience shaming or are

---

8. Richard Rohr, *The Universal Christ* (New York: Convergent Press/Penguin Random House, 2019), 16.

9. Ibid., 15. Emphasis in the original.

10. Shroyer, *Original Blessing,* 24.

told of our unworthiness, we can look within ourselves (and even the person(s) spewing the hate) with grace and through the lens of belovedness. If the sum of your existence was boiled down to one thing, it would be the truth that you and I, everyone in your sociology class, your bedraggled biology professor, your pot-luck first-year roommate, your family, and everyone you know . . . are blessed and beloved. You are made very good. Sin and all.

What We Talk about When We Talk about "Love"

Again, why write about belovedness and why does this matter in college? Because underneath the questions of vocation, relationships, and navigating young adulthood is the question, "Who am I?" I want you to believe wholeheartedly that belovedness is the innermost "I am" of your identity in God. It is the essence of your soul. It is also belonging. Because I am beloved, I belong to God. I belong to something bigger than I could ever comprehend. "Beloved" means there is a lover and an object of that love. God, the Trinity[11] (the one described earlier as pure relationship), is bound by eternal love flowing from one to the other. In fact, any time someone asks of God's name, the response is never a name but instead an attribute, an essence. God says to Moses, "I AM" (Exod. 3:13–15) and later in a whole bunch of places, God is described as: "slow to anger, abounding in steadfast love."[12] The author of the First Letter of John writes: "God is love" (1 John 4:8). But what kind of love are we talking about here? The Greek language (in which the New Testament was written by the early church) has four words for our one English word meaning "love."[13] *Storge* love is an empathetic love like the love we have when we see a baby or a golden-doodle. *Philia* love is the love felt between friends or siblings and deeply appreciates the gift of another's friendship. *Eros* love is the romantic, pleasure, sensual, and sexual

---

11. Traditionally the Trinity is known as the Father, Son, and Holy Spirit. See Richard Rohr's *The Divine Dance* for more.

12. See Exodus 34, Numbers 14, Psalm 86, Psalm 103, and Psalm 130.

13. There are more than four—some say as many as six—different types of love. In *The Four Loves*, C. S. Lewis focuses on these four: *storge, philia, eros,* and *agape.*

love of passion. Lastly, *agape* love is the unconditional, charitable, and unchanging love of God for humanity. Belovedness is the *agape* love of God for the object of love—us. In the Old Testament, the Hebrew word for this love means something like "loving-kindness"—but more on this in chapter 6.

We want to reclaim this *agape* love, this loving-kindness as belovedness, for college students, and we want you to claim it for yourselves. College is the perfect time, developmentally and formationally, to practice this belovedness as a foundation for how you live your life long after you turn the tassel. We think this understanding of ourselves and the world has the power to transform the experience of college into a positive one, filled with joy—even amidst brokenness.

College can be like playing Jenga˚ with my two-year-old daughter: you've spent time carefully stacking (or maybe someone stacked them for you) the blocks, which are your beliefs, only to have the tower utterly demolished. What blocks are left standing? Don't get me wrong, I'm not equating intellectualism or academia with my destructive toddler, but rather that college is naturally a time of deconstruction. In your independence, it's a time to figure out what you think you know and believe to be true.[14] However, one block will remain no matter how many times you or life tries to kick it over: the block with "*agape*," "blessed," "very goodness," and "belovedness" written all over it. As Paul writes in a prayer for a community he began in Ephesus: "that Christ may dwell in your hearts through faith, as you are being rooted and grounded in love" (Eph. 3:17). Christ's love for you is the grounding when it seems like all we thought was foundational is in ruins. It is here, when identity and vocation seem to be up in the air, belovedness is the voice beckoning us to return home to the one who chases us with love.

When the voice opened up from heaven to say to Jesus, "This is my beloved," it was the beginning of love coming to dwell with us. You are in

---

14. Note: I'm not saying "belief and doubt" because, to doubt and wrestle is holy, natural, and transformative. Talk of beliefs is boring. Now is the time to experience for yourself what is most true and good in this world? How will what you find build your moral character?

Christ, therefore you too are called beloved. You too are called to dwell in that love.

Campus Holy Ground

Belovedness is sacramental. ("Sacramental" is just a churchy way of saying "an outward and visible sign of an inward grace," which also comes from the same word that means "holy" or "set apart.") If we treat others as though they are already beloved (which they are), then it creates a space of belonging for someone else. It shows as a visible sign of something often invisible. In my church, when someone is baptized, we all profess to "seek and serve Christ in all persons."[15] I love this part of the baptism because it's like we are being challenged to see and respect someone else's belovedness. On campus, it is important to find space that demonstrates *agape* love and belonging.

One of my favorite bible verses (and definitions of who Jesus Christ is) comes from Colossians 1:15. It says Jesus is the visible "image of an invisible God." In other words, Jesus himself is a sacrament for the world to see and experience the grace and love of the Godhead. Jesus frequently told his followers, "Whoever has seen me has seen the Father" (John 14:9).

So for us to become a sacramental space on campus, we have to create community that is a visible sign of grace. We cannot become that place of belonging if we're telling folks "who is in and who is out." We cannot become that visible place of grace if we're excluding another of God's beloved children. We are not reflecting *agape* love, loving-kindness, original blessing, or belovedness if we're exiling LGBTQ+ folks, for example.

Beloved, sacramental space is a nonconforming space. It does not judge or evaluate or quantify or perform. Instead, it is a place of vulnerability. It is different and challenges the feel of other spaces on campus. It is set apart—as in, fully engaged with the world around it—yet not conforming to the norms the world says are important. You could even call this space *holy*.

---

15. The Book of Common Prayer, 305.

It is in this free space that veneers of performance and expectations are broken down and vulnerability allows us to share our stories, our faith, our doubts, our lives. My mentor and boss, Bishop Anne Hodges-Copple, says of college students, "Sometimes it's not easy to say, 'Yes, I'm a Christian,' but if we do, we then say, 'But please don't ask me to talk about Jesus.'" This holy space is not a place to compartmentalize your faith or belief in God but instead a place to practice—to go inward. It is a space we can and should wrestle: with God, with scripture in all its messiness and grace, with theology (meaning "God-talk"), and with how it intersects with academia and science. Ideally, we would call this place "church," but we all know that church is a loaded word and unfortunately many churches create an atmosphere of fear or are egocentric—like a performance rather than a space of worship.

On campus you will need authentic spaces to nurture your soul, make room for healthy skepticism, and wrestle with scripture. After all, wisdom is gained through forgiveness, questioning, practicing love in action, and wrestling with God. To expound upon that earlier saying of Jean Vanier, wisdom and transformation in a Christian campus setting come through *practicing belovedness* as flawed people in an imperfect community. Christian campus community is a school not only of love but of *wisdom* as you experience your holy awakening.

Awakening to Your Inherent Value

One of the greatest stories of belonging, one that is central to understanding the nature of the *agape* love of God, comes straight from Jesus's mouth. It is the story of awakening through a moment of an epiphany or "coming to your senses." In Luke chapter 15, Jesus tells three parables of lost things: a lost sheep, a lost coin, and lost people. In this last parable, commonly known as the parable of the prodigal son, this awakening is precisely what happens to the younger son (read: college student) who leaves home, makes bad choices, comes to his senses, and encounters theophany—something unexpected.

John Dominic Crossan says that a parable is a "metaphorical story." This particular parable is an "example" parable where Jesus likens the nature of God as cosmic love, acceptance, and forgiveness—all through the simple act of storytelling.[16] The Hebrew name for this type of storytelling is *meshalim* ("wisdom storytelling through parable or proverb of careful comparison to prove a point"). The root word of *meshalim* is *meshal,* meaning "be like." So in Luke 15:11–32, Jesus reveals much about our need to awaken to the reality of God who "be like" a loving parent.

> There was a man who had two sons. The younger of them said to his father, "Father, give me the share of the property that will belong to me." So he divided his property between them. A few days later the younger son gathered all he had and traveled to a distant country, and there he squandered his property in dissolute living. When he had spent everything, a severe famine took place in that country, and he began to be in need. So he went and hired himself out to one of the citizens of that country, who sent him to his fields to feed the pigs. He would gladly have filled himself with the pods that the pigs were eating; and no one gave him anything. *But when he came to himself* he said, "How many of my father's hired hands have bread enough and to spare, but here I am dying of hunger! I will get up and go to my father, and I will say to him, 'Father, I have sinned against heaven and before you; I am no longer worthy to be called your son; treat me like one of your hired hands.'" So he set off and went to his father. But while he was still far off, his father saw him and was filled with compassion; he ran and put his arms around him and kissed him. Then the son said to him, "Father, I have sinned against heaven and before you; I am no longer worthy to be called your son." But the father said to his slaves, "Quickly, bring out a robe—the best one— and put it on him; put a ring on his finger and sandals on his feet. And get the fattened calf and kill it, and let us eat and celebrate; for this son of mine was dead and is alive again; he was lost and is found!" And they began to celebrate.

Did you catch that? The son "comes to his senses." He remembers. He awakens to the love that was already and always there. He's sorry and

---

16. John Dominic Crossan, *The Power of Parables* (New York: Harper Collins, 2012), 6–10.

seeks forgiveness (because that is what you do when you hurt people who love you.) One of my favorite theologians, Diogenes Allen, says this passage reveals "that God takes each of us very seriously, far more seriously than we take ourselves. Each of us is so valuable to God that God seeks to find and to welcome us into his glorious kingdom."[17] He goes further to say that this notion of God loving us would have been radical to people who are accustomed to appeasing angry, egocentric gods. The image of the father running (people didn't run in those days where running meant hiking up his garment), revealing his man-thighs, would have been ridiculous. The "deeply insulted father who rushes out to welcome his wastrel son . . . introduced something that was utterly new to the entire world. No one had ever taught that every person is of imperishable value."[18] Prodigal means "extravagant." At the outset of the parable we see the younger son as extravagant in his magnificent spending of his inheritance/retirement-come-early. But by the end, it is the father's love and forgiveness that are lavish and abundant. Jewish listeners would have instantly connected this to "loving-kindness" and the "very-goodness" of God's blessing. Other parables offer glimpses of who God is, but this one (and the other two stories of lost things) reveal that God is not interested in religion or our repentance but desires us in relationship. The God of the cosmos stands on the precipice of the kingdom (which is "very near" to you—as close as a heartbeat) waiting, loving, calling.

Conclusion

This notion of our inherent value to God can be overwhelming. Learning that there is nothing you or I could do that would make God love us less is mind-blowing, heart-in-the-throat news. Because this is the best news. You are precious to God and no one can ever take it from you. So perhaps it's time to drop the other identities and lean into your beloved-

---

17. Diogenes Allen, *Theology for a Troubled Believer: An Introduction to Christian Faith* (Louisville, KY: Westminster John Knox Press, 2010), xxi.

18. Ibid.

ness. I'm thinking of the social identifications and monikers that worked for a while—whether it's Greek life or service club or the premed crowd. Nothing is wrong with these circles, but they do not define you. Your belonging is wrapped up in something much deeper. As Psalm 42:7 says, "Deep calls out to deep." The high school "clique" of belonging kicked the can of identity down the road to college and here you are.

When you show up on campus, you're still a high schooler until some point during your first year when you awaken to the change in your being. The journey for you as a young adult has begun. The frontiers of joy and heartbreak, acceptance and rejection, identity and identity crisis await you. Wherever you are on the spectrum of believing you are beloved, let's just imagine (for the sake of this book) that this is true. It is Truth with a capital "T." Can we agree to accept this basic and yet complicated truth long enough to begin to see how it can shape our actions, how we see people, and how we move through college? It is our hope that you will emerge an integrated and whole person with this same sense of wonder. It is our hope that long after college, you go on to create beloved community wherever you are.

Belovedness can weather suffering, band together for a greater cause, bring happiness to the isolated, and bring wholeness to all. It creates belonging and fulfills our longing and desire for deep connection. When we live from our belovedness, we see the belovedness of others and become the body of Christ.

> **Going Deeper** Throughout this chapter (in the footnotes), you'll see the books and theologians who influenced my thinking about belovedness. Call me old-fashioned, but I turn to books when I'm searching for answers to questions like, "Who am I?" In addition to the previously cited books, I would recommend the following resources on your journey of awakening to a greater understanding of who you are:

- Donald Miller's *Blue Like Jazz: Nonreligious Thoughts on Christian Spirituality* (Thomas Nelson, 2003). A hilarious memoir of coming-of-age-in-college, Miller discovers a new understanding of God's love and what it means to be Christian in college. I read this during my own crisis of faith in college and it had a profound impact.

- Brendan Manning's *The Ragamuffin Gospel: Good News for the Bedraggled, Beat-Up, and Burnt Out* (Multnomah, 1990). In this groundbreaking book, Manning tells the story of his own awakening to God's grace. Worth the read!

- No time to read (because, college)? Try these podcasts: Pete Enn's *The Bible for Normal People*; *The Liturgists Podcast*; Rob Bell's *The RobCast; Another Name for Every Thing with Richard Rohr*; and *The Bible Binge*.

CHAPTER 2

MAKING CHOICES

Stacy Alan

In the beloved movie *The Princess Bride*, a swordsman, who had spent his whole life preparing to exact revenge on a six-fingered villain, says the following immortal words: "Hello. My name is Íñigo Montoya. You killed my father. Prepare to die." Tragedy had marked him at an early age and his purpose in life was clear: avenge the death of his father. Íñigo's purpose had been imposed on him. He had a plan and he followed it doggedly.

Many of us long for that kind of clarity—albeit without the tragedy. Wouldn't it be nice to know for sure what I'm supposed to do with my life, with whom, and what for? This chapter is an exploration of what we in the church business call *discernment*.

What's Wrong with a Plan?

"God has a plan for your life." This is the title of at least one Christian self-help book and the subtitle of countless more. There are workshops, webpages, lists of Bible verses, and blogposts—all of them offering advice, assurances, and admonition about how to figure out what God has in mind for you. Many of these resources cite Jeremiah 29:11: "For surely I know the plans I have for you, says the LORD, plans for your welfare and not for harm, to give you a future with hope."

If you pay attention to the text, however, you might notice something that I'd like you to keep in mind as you keep reading. Jeremiah quotes God saying "I know the plans I have for you": "plans" is plural. What might it mean to understand that God has *plans* for you, rather than a plan? What would it mean to know that discernment is a dialogue rather than simply conforming to a plan?

For many folks, the idea of God having a plan for their life is comforting. In the midst of so very many options and choices—relationships, careers, religious affiliation, values, political engagement—to believe that someone, anyone, knows what's supposed to happen can be a relief. All I have to do is pray and watch and listen for God's guidance. Then I'll know. For many, however, the initial comfort gives way to a nagging worry: What if I get it wrong? What if I'm not praying correctly? What if I mishear God's call? But really, WHAT IF I GET IT WRONG? Will God be angry? Disappointed? Will my life be ruined? Will I be judged or abandoned by the God who is supposed to love me?

Then, when things go wrong (notice I say "when," not "if"), is that a sign that I have failed?[1] That I have gotten God wrong?

You Keep Using That Word ...

The word that is often used to talk about this process of figuring out what ideas God has about what one should do with one's life is *discernment*. For many people the word "discernment" means figuring out whether one is called to ordained ministry in the church, to be a pastor or a priest. Discernment, however, is something all of us do. It's about getting clarity about what God is calling each of us to do with our whole life, all of those things I listed above.

It's kind of a cliché to go to the dictionary definition and etymology of a word but bear with me. In this case it's helpful to sweep away some unhelpful churchy baggage. The word "discern" comes from two Latin roots: *dis-* "apart" + *cernere* "to separate" and its dictionary definition (according to Merriam-Webster) includes: "to detect with the eyes or with senses other than vision, to recognize or identify as separate and distinct, to come to know or recognize mentally, and to see or understand the difference." In these senses, discernment isn't so much about figuring out a puzzle, or solving a mystery, but rather clearing away what isn't good or true or important—separating out—so that we may

---

1. See chapter 3 on "Success and Failure" for advice on how to avoid failing. Just kidding. You will fail. And you will be OK. More than OK. You will still be beloved.

recognize what has been before us all along: what is good, and true, and important.

Another word that I've already been using is the word "call." In the church you might also hear the word "vocation." They are essentially synonyms, since the word "vocation" comes from the Latin verb "to call." I prefer to use God's "call" or "vocation" rather than God's plan, for all of the reasons I've outlined above. A plan is static, fixed, a mandate—I either fit myself into it, or I don't.

"Hello. My Name Is Íñigo … of Loyola. Prepare to Live."

At the beginning of the sixteenth century, a young man named Ignatius asked similar questions about his life.[2] In his early adulthood, Ignatius seemed to have a clear sense of his life plan: to party, fight, and rise in the ranks of the court—and thereby become famous. According to one biography:

> Winning personal glory was his passion. He was a fancy dresser, an expert dancer, a womanizer, sensitive to insult, and a rough punkish swordsman who used his privileged status to escape prosecution for violent crimes committed with his priest brother at carnival time.[3]

In 1521 he was gravely injured in a battle with the French. His right leg was shattered and he was carried home to Loyola. His vanity was such that when the leg healed crooked, he had it rebroken and reset—in an age when there were no anesthetics.

Over his long convalescence, Ignatius spent time daydreaming and reading the only two books at hand, *The Life of Christ* and a book of stories about the saints. Here we get a hint of one of the most important

---

2. While he is known now as Ignatius of Loyola, *Princess Bride* fans will be interested to know that his given name was Íñigo, and, while a six-fingered man didn't kill his father, Ignatius's passion and focus were not too unlike those of Íñigo Montoya.

3. George Traub and Debra Mooney, "A Biography of St. Ignatius Loyola," Xavier University, accessed November 4, 2019, www.xavier.edu/jesuitresource/understanding -our-heritage/life-of-ignatius/ignatius-biography.

aspects of discernment: paying attention. When he daydreamed, he fantasized about acts of chivalry:

> He pictured to himself what he should do in honor of an illustrious lady, how he should journey to the city where she was, in what words he would address her, and what bright and pleasant sayings he would make use of, what manner of warlike exploits he should perform to please her. He was so carried away by this thought that he did not even perceive how far beyond his power it was to do what he proposed.[4]

As he spent more time reading about the life of Christ and about the saints, the feats he fantasized about became more and more about these holy heroes:

> While perusing the life of Our Lord and the saints, he began to reflect, saying to himself: "What if I should do what St. Francis did?" "What if I should act like St. Dominic?" He pondered over these things in his mind, and kept continually proposing to himself serious and difficult things.[5]

As the days and weeks went on, he noticed something. He still would daydream of feats of bravery and chivalry, as well as of acts of holiness and self-denial, and he would still enjoy them, but the aftereffects were different:

> This succession of thoughts occupied him for a long while, those about God alternating with those about the world. But in these thoughts there was this difference. When he thought of worldly things it gave him great pleasure, but afterward he found himself dry and sad. But when he thought of journeying to Jerusalem, and of living only on herbs, and practising austerities, he found pleasure not only while thinking of them, but also when he had ceased.[6]

---

4. Ignatius of Loyola, *The Autobiography of St. Ignatius*, ed. J. F. X. O'Conor (New York: Benziger Brothers, 1900), 25–26.

5. Ibid., 26.

6. Ibid., 26–27.

This insight was the beginning of a journey for Ignatius that changed his entire life. When he finally recovered, he literally hung up his sword and developed one of the most powerful programs of prayer and discernment in Western Christianity, *The Spiritual Exercises*. He ended up inspiring both men and women to listen prayerfully for and discern God's call in their lives.[7]

After his conversion, Ignatius took all of the passion he had invested in romance, military glory, and fame and channeled it into his love affair with Christ. It demanded his all: his best efforts, his deepest love, his most courageous honesty. Ignatius understood his call to be part of a cosmic struggle, the forces of God and good against the forces of evil.

Despite, or perhaps because, of God's absolute love for you, careful, prayerful discernment is vitally important and requires our best efforts. For one, the world is in desperate need of people who are fully engaged with the ways in which God can use their unique gifts and experiences and passions to bring about healing, wholeness, justice, and peace. The powers of evil—the forces that Ignatius simply calls the enemy of our human nature—conspire to keep us unfree and focused on the wrong things. God has invited us to be part of God's work of healing and redeeming humanity, and through us, all of creation.[8]

"I'm No One to Be Trifled With."

The first step, before we can truly hear God's call, is to understand who we truly are. The premise of this entire book is that you are a beloved child of God. This was Ignatius's understanding as well, something he articulated in the very first meditation in his *Spiritual Exercises,* called the "Principle and Foundation." It is dry with entire chapters written on just this part, but here we'll just scratch the surface:

> God created human beings to praise, reverence, and serve God, and by doing this, to save their souls.

---

7. He also founded the religious order of the Jesuits, which grew and quickly spread, sending missionaries and founding schools around the world within his lifetime.

8. Romans 8:19–23.

God created all other things on the face of the earth to help fulfill this purpose.

From this it follows that we are to use the things of this world only to the extent that they help us to this end, and we ought to rid ourselves of the things of this world to the extent that they get in the way of this end.

For this it is necessary to make ourselves indifferent to all created things as much as we are able, . . . so that we ultimately desire and choose only what is most conducive for us to the end for which God created us.[9]

Ignatius uses the concepts and language of his day, which sometimes need a little translation. The first thing Ignatius says is that humans were created "to praise, reverence, and serve God." That is, to be in relationship with God, recognizing that God is God, God is good, and God created us out of love. The second thing he says is that it is this relationship that "saves our souls." Today we would probably say something like "become our truest and best selves." The rest of the Principle and Foundation states that *all* of creation is good and is at our disposal to help us become our best selves in relation to God and each other.[10] In Ignatius's era it was assumed that it was automatically better to be a nun or a monk or a priest than, say, to be married or a weaver or a tradesperson, so this understanding of ourselves as beloved creatures in a beloved creation gives us a profound freedom to find our truest selves in the broadest sense possible.

Some of us enter adulthood—whether it's starting college or a training program, or getting a job, or a gap year, or something else—with a whole backpack of expectations and assumptions from other people. A

---

9. You can find a wonderfully updated paraphrase of the Principle and Foundation written by David Fleming, SJ, by simply doing an internet search for "Principal and Foundation" and "Fleming." See https://www.bc.edu/content/dam/files/offices/ministry/pdf/First%20Principle%20and%20Foundation%20-March%202015%20%282%29.pdf.

10. Some raise the question of whether this means that the rest of creation exists only for our benefit, without its own inherent goodness and belovedness. I would say that God's relationship to the rest of creation is unknown to us. What Ignatius is trying to do here is remind us of the freedom each of us has within the created order.

scientific career might not seem to be an option because I'm female. I might have been told that rich, fulfilling relationships are not possible because I'm asexual. Choosing a satisfying but relatively low-paying career may seem to be off the table because my family is anxious about money. Ignatius says that anything[11] is an option to consider as I explore God's call.

The key is in Ignatius's first insight from his sick bed: *paying attention*. Discernment does include practical things like lists of pros and cons, considering my commitments and the needs of people I'm accountable to, but it's also about paying attention to where I find joy,[12] where I am restless, what doesn't sit right, where my energy is. Like Ignatius on his sick bed, noting the empty feeling after some daydreams and the energy and enjoyment that lasted after others, it's about noticing when some activities are life-giving and which, even when enjoyable, are life-draining. It's about attending to the places where you perceive God in your everyday life and noticing when you seem to have drifted away. It's about listening for Jesus's call to you through the stories of the Gospels. It's about allowing the Spirit to guide you in prayer, using all of your faculties: ideas, emotions, memories, imagination, intuition.

"You Only Think I Guessed Wrong!"

One incident has always stood out to me as an important clue to how to understand discernment. Once Ignatius recovered, he pledged to make a pilgrimage to Jerusalem and within two years made the difficult journey to the Holy Land. A short time after arriving, he is ordered to leave under pain of excommunication and he returned to Spain, deciding that God had not intended him to stay in the Holy Land, but that he was now supposed to continue his education so that he could "be better fitted to save souls."

---

11. As long as it's not inherently immoral or unjust.

12. Joy is not the same as happiness. Joy, which is similar to something Ignatius called consolation, is about rightness—right relationship, right ends and right means, right intention—whereas happiness, while nice, is a temporary state of good feelings, which can lead us astray.

The dream of returning to Jerusalem never completely left Ignatius, however, and later in life, when he had gathered a group of men[13] around him who had caught his vision (the "companions"), they attempted more than once to go there together. Ignatius was never successful.

What did this mean? He truly believed that God was calling him to the Holy Land. Had he discerned wrong? Getting it wrong, perhaps, isn't the way to think about it. The dream of traveling to Jerusalem had been part of his conversion, a goal that lay ahead and drew him beyond himself. His time in Jerusalem had been spiritually rich, and the journey there had taught him about developing a profound trust in and dependence on God. In his autobiography, he never expresses regret for the original journey, nor anxiety about the return being unsuccessful.

Perhaps discernment isn't so much about getting things "right," but rather about being faithful. It won't always be easy: we may need to shift the vision as we go, we may encounter resistance that requires us to stop and discern again whether we are still following God or have been pulled astray. We may need to listen carefully to the voices of others, some of whom have wisdom we need and others of whom may be in error. In the end, all God really wants is for you to turn God-ward so that you can do this work together.

"As You Wish ..."

So now I get to God's secret plan. (You thought we'd left plans behind, didn't you?) When I talk about Ignatius's understandings of prayer and discernment, many people get excited about the discernment part. They—understandably—want to know what they should do with their lives; they want to be faithful and free and fully themselves. Discernment is indeed important. It is something that requires intention and work. But I have come to understand that the work of discernment is God's holy bait and switch, a way of drawing us closer. In order to do discernment well, we have to learn to be in relationship with God. We need

---

13. While Ignatius's companions and the future Jesuit order were comprised only of men, he had an active and intellectually engaged correspondence with several women.

to spend time in God's presence, conversing and sitting silently in each other's presence, telling God what we most desire and allowing God to share what is closest to God's heart. And more than having us discern well, God wants simply to be with us.

In the *Exercises*, Ignatius says something striking:

> A step or two in front of the place where I am to contemplate or meditate, I will stand for the length of an Our Father, raising my mind above and considering how God our Lord is looking at me, etc., and make an act of reverence or humility (Exx. 75).[14]

Robert Marsh, SJ, calls this "looking at God looking at me."[15] To discern means to spend time being aware that God sees me as a beloved creature, in all of my glory and my flaws. The work of discernment is one of the ways that God woos us, inviting us into work together so that we may fall head over heels in love with the God who loved us first. This is God's desire for us.

This is why, as important as careful discernment is, in a fundamental way, you can't get it wrong. God is inviting you into an epic love affair—more epic, I dare say, than *The Princess Bride*[16]—one that will make you most truly yourself, demand your best for the sake of building God's reign of peace and justice, and set you free. We can now return to that oft-quoted line from Jeremiah: "For surely I know the plans I have for you, says the LORD, plans for your welfare and not for harm, to give you a future with hope." God has all kinds of plans for you—for us—plans that you get to have a say in, plans that will draw you forward, plans for all of our good.

---

14. Ignatius of Loyola, *The Spiritual Exercises*, trans. Elder Mullan, SJ (New York: P.J. Kenedy & Sons, 1914), 26.

15. Robert Marsh, SJ, "Looking at God, Looking at You: Ignatius' Third Addition," *The Way* 43, no. 4 (October 2004): 19–28.

16. Or whatever story makes your heart soar, your heart race, your breath catch, and your eyes glisten.

"Then Wove,Twue Wove,Will Follow You Fowever ..."

When my son, who happens to be named after Ignatius, was four years old, he wandered up into the pulpit of a church we were visiting. I was chatting with a friend and when I noticed him up there, I called out to him, "What does Mommy say when she's up there?" He raised one hand dramatically and said, "God loves you. Pay attention!"

The Impressive Clergyman in the *Princess Bride* attempts to make a declaration about love and is thwarted by the evil prince. But the love that calls us in the work of discernment cannot, will not, be thwarted, and will also follow us, assuring us, if we are paying attention, that we are never alone and that we are never abandoned.

And there you have it. Discernment is both the simplest and most challenging thing you'll ever do, a task for the rest of your life: remember, first and foremost, God loves you—absolutely and irrevocably—and desires you to be most fully the person you were created to be. In order to do that, in order to be the most loving, faithful, fulfilled, fruitful version of that self, you must pay attention; a skill that must be used and honed so that you can see the powerful and miraculous ways that God works with each of us to bring to fulfillment—not God's plan, but rather God's dream.

God loves you. Pay attention.

Going Deeper You probably started this chapter expecting, or at least hoping, that I would provide some tried-and-true techniques guaranteed to bring you clarity about God's will. You'll notice, now that you've come to the end, that there were no to-do lists, no charts or graphs, no 5-point plans. That was on purpose. I wanted you to realize that this was, first and last, about the love affair between you and God. If you are ready to do some concrete discernment about specific questions in your life, I highly recommend the following resources:

Elizabeth Liebert's *The Way of Discernment: Spiritual Practices for Decision Making* (Westminster John Knox Press, 2008). In it she guides you through various prayer techniques for discernment, many of them in the Ignatian tradition, plus several more. She talks about the importance of forming the question and, in the range of prayer practices, honors the many ways that we pray.

Dean Brackley's *The Call to Discernment in Troubled Times: New Perspectives on the Transformative Wisdom of Ignatius of Loyola* (Crossroad, 2004). Brackley takes the reader through Ignatius's process of discernment, with a strong connection between this kind of discernment and the work for social justice. He joined the staff of the *Universidad Centroamericana* in El Salvador after the assassination of the six Jesuits there in 1989, and this book was profoundly formed by that experience. It is deep stuff and stands up to multiple readings.

Pierre Wolff's *Discernment: The Art of Choosing Well, Based on Ignatian Spirituality* (Ligouri, 1993, 2003). While less comprehensive in terms of techniques than Liebert's book, it goes deep into the Ignatian mode of discernment and honors both the head and the heart in the process. It's also a lot shorter than Brackley's book, so a good way to get started. He also gives guidelines for doing discernment as an individual and with the support of a group.

www.ignatianspirituality.com. A wonderful collection of resources in the Ignatian tradition, with a wide range of contributors.

The *Observatio*, which is a prayer resource. See appendix.

CHAPTER 3

SUCCESS AND FAILURE

Brandon Harris

Around late September, a first-year student stopped by my office with tears in his eyes. I invited him to sit down for a cup of coffee. He sat down with a loud sigh and buried his face into both palms. "I don't know if this major is going to work. I failed my first exam, and I don't understand this subject, but I don't want my parents to think I'm a failure." His statement was followed by a cascade of doubts: "If I don't pass this class, I won't get into this club on campus, and you know how competitive those are. I want to be successful, like my brother, who's a senior. I want the right internship, the perfect study abroad opportunity, and the right job."

We place a dizzying amount of pressure on ourselves to succeed. We all want to make something out of ourselves, and we do the best we can with this one wild and glorious life. However, our desire for success can lead to tremendous pressures as we force ourselves to push past our capacities. We exhaust ourselves trying to craft the perfect resume, the right life narrative, and the perfectly curated Instagram. The world around us only reinforces the pressures to succeed. Memes that state "I grind while you sleep" strengthen the narrative that to be successful is to be exhausted. Our families pressure us to follow family traditions to attend particular colleges or choose a major that they deem as acceptable. The pressure to succeed is reinforced by comparing ourselves to friends and classmates who seem to have it all together. Like Drake, we sing, "I just wanna be successful." What happens when we fail? What happens when the perfectly curated life we imagined for ourselves doesn't quite happen the way we expect? What are we to make of failure? This chapter will explore success and failure in light of the way of Jesus.

The good news is this: there will be moments of success and failure. It is not our successes or our failures that define ourselves and our lives, but who we are as children of God. This chapter will explore success, failure, and holding our triumphs and disappointments as lessons on our journey with God.

Success

"Congratulations!" those words ring out across the top of the acceptance letter. "You've been accepted to college!" All the years of late nights, striving for the right grades, extracurricular activities, and volunteer hours have led to this moment. Have you ever accomplished something, or been told you were successful but wondered what the point of success is in the first place? What are we to make of it and do with it?

In my childhood I was taught an old poem called "Invictus" by William Ernest Henley. He closes this poem with these lines:

> It matters not how strait the gate,
> How charged with punishments the scroll,
> I am the master of my fate,
> I am the captain of my soul.[1]

This poem has offered inspiration and meaning to luminaries such as Nelson Mandela, to college sophomores pledging a fraternity, and parents seeking to inspire their children. Despite the popularity of this poem, quite frankly, I don't believe it. "I am the master of my fate"—are we? Are we the captains of our soul? Mastery of life and control of our destinies is the approach to life that we are taught from a young age. College only reinforces the idea that we must master and control our life experiences. We must choose the right major, the perfect internship, and we must join exclusive clubs, fraternities, or sororities. We are led to believe that our life's purpose is the pursuit of the next objective. Life quickly becomes a long to-do list of accomplishments we must meet.

1.William Ernest Henley, "Invictus by William Ernest Henley," Poetry Foundation, accessed August 9, 2019, www.poetryfoundation.org/poems/51642/invictus.

The belief that we are the masters of our fate places an unfair burden upon our shoulders. That way of thinking, this philosophy of life, places an excessive amount of pressure on us. This way of living is exhausting as we run ourselves ragged. We try to keep ourselves from making mistakes, from failing, from breaking out of our tightly wound boxes because we believe that we have to control our lives. It doesn't help that you can compare your life to everyone else's at every moment on Instagram or Snapchat. So we begin to believe the lie. We believe that we need to grab control of the reins of life; we need to master our souls and our fates and take charge. The running narrative in our minds is that our mastery of each moment defines a successful college career. The myth is handed to us that we need to push ourselves, grab every opportunity, stay up all night, join every club, volunteer ceaselessly, get the right major, score internships, and get the right job after college, and we will be successful!

Don't get me wrong here: I know we all want to make something of our lives, to produce something of worth and value, to accomplish goals and tasks. The pursuit of success is essential. We should want to do things with excellence, to try our best, to use the gifts, talents, and skills we possess for a larger purpose. It is natural for us to long for meaningful lives. However, our success lies not in our continuous striving for piles of accolades, awards, likes, and doing everything correctly. We often find that those successes leave us empty, longing, and wandering for more. The way of Jesus offers us another way. The way of Jesus invites us into a narrative that does not define success as how much we produce or accomplish but in lives marked with peace, love, and joy.[2]

In the Gospel of Mark,[3] Jesus sends out the twelve disciples to preach, to cast out evil spirits, and to proclaim the beginning of a new kingdom. When they returned, they were full of stories of the accomplishments that occurred, the successes had, and of the marvelous things they had witnessed. Jesus, in response to all of their achievements, invites them to step away from it all and to rest. The invitation from Jesus at that moment was to put the disciples' feats into perspective. By stepping

---

2. Galatians 5:22–23.
3. Mark 6:7–13.

back, the disciples were able to witness their lives as a complete whole. Their achievements were defined not merely by what they did but also their need for love, for rest, and wholeness. The disciples were invited to live new lives, in which their identity was not marked by the applause of those who had witnessed their victory. Instead, the invitation to rest was an invitation to develop a new identity.

Love, joy, and peace are manifestations of an inward groundedness. Novelist and Presbyterian minister Frederick Buechner writes, "Power, success, happiness, as the world knows them, are his who will fight for them hard enough; but peace, love, joy are only from God."[4] We are invited to participate in a journey with God. Our lives are grand adventures, miraculous and ordinary, open to twists and turns. Within that adventure, we will find success along the way. Like the disciples, we must step away for a while, to examine our success for what it is.

Humility

Jesus's invitation for the disciples to rest after accomplishing such great feats is a reminder to view ourselves with humility. We are human; created for joy, not merely boundless striving, constant work, and needless plodding throughout our life. Our deeds are not solely the byproducts of our efforts. Humility enables us to view our achievements as a piece of the puzzle that is our lives. We are invited to hold our success a little more loosely, because it is only a fraction of the larger whole.

Humility, frankly, is a confusing concept. The Merriam-Webster Dictionary defines it as freedom from pride or arrogance. Being humble is an admirable quality; of course, we don't want to be prideful or arrogant. But what are we to do with humility? What is the balance between being modest and also making space for the fact that we are gifted and talented individuals who are striving for success?

Humility is often presented as self-deprecation, as a way of not owning the efforts we have placed in reaching our goals or desires. It is

---

4.F rederick Buechner, "The Magnificent Defeat," Day 1, last modified November 7, 2014, http://day1.org/6297-the_magnificent_defeat.

neither self-deprecating or being overly modest about our lives. The Christian tradition places humility as a virtue to be treasured, a means of freedom for our souls, and a guide on our journey through life. It is an invitation to live in awe that there is a larger narrative in which we are participants. Humility as a virtue invites us into the knowing that life is not dependent upon our mastery of it but on our dependence on the love and mercy of God. There is a larger narrative, a grand sweep of human history in which our lives play a part. It is the story of God's love at work within the world through time, place, and the lives of ordinary individuals. Humility is the conscious recognition of being loved by God and that we are neither as important as we imagine ourselves to be or as insignificant as we fear ourselves to be. We are deeply loved and known by a God who scripture tells us knows the very number of hairs on our head.[5]

Henri Nouwen, a noted Catholic priest and author writes, "Often we are made to believe that self-deprecation is a virtue, called humility. But humility is in reality the opposite of self-deprecation. It is the grateful recognition that we are precious in God's eyes and that all we are is a pure gift."[6] Modesty is not self-effacing; there's no need to take shots at yourself. Simultaneously, humility liberates us from the pressure of believing that our lives are dependent upon ourselves rather than God's conscious participation and action within us and around us. We are invited to stand in awe of a God who loves us, who works through us and for us and avails God-self to us. When we live with modesty, we can celebrate our accomplishments and success. We can step away from our work to rest, to be renewed, and to remember that who we are is not merely what we can produce or accomplish. Humility allows us to hold our triumphs loosely, not needing to feel the pressure that everything depends upon our efforts and work. Humility is also the gateway virtue, keeping not only our success but our failures.

---

5. Luke 12:7.

6. Henri Nouwen, "Growing Beyond Self-Rejection," Henri Nouwen Society, accessed August 9, 2019, https://henrinouwen.org/meditation/growing-beyond-self -rejection/

Failure

I stood there holding my breath as my intro to political theory professor leaned back in his chair. His brow furrowed, his hands pressed against his lips. He took a deep breath and exhaled, "Mr. Harris. I expect more out of you. Today was your first exam in this class, and you failed. Not only did you fail, but I can also tell you didn't try." I couldn't believe this conversation was happening. I had never failed an exam and I always performed reasonably well in high school. So far, my freshman year had gone well, until now. Here I was in my professor's office having failed an exam. He leaned forward in his chair, "Mr. Harris, don't you ever fail one of my exams again." A cloud of shame accompanied me as I walked to my dorm that afternoon. My sense of worth and identity was tied to my academic performance. I faced failure for the first time in college that day, and I wasn't sure what to do.

Inevitably, we will fail on this human journey, whether it is an exam or class, a project, an internship, or our expectations or the opinions of others. Failure is bound to meet us on the road to life, yet we are so afraid of failure. We do everything possible to avoid it, and then when we fail, we allow that moment to mark our sense of identity and worth. We wear failure like a heavy load of groceries we're carrying up a hill. Disaster is a load on our minds that haunts us, and we replay the moment over and over in our minds, asking ourselves what we could have done differently. We wonder what our parents, friends, or family would think if they knew we bombed. We look to mask our failures. No one, after all, goes around sharing their fiascos on their Instastories.

If we view failure in this way, we will miss the ways that it can speak to us. Failure is a chance to become aware of our human limitations. It is a reminder of our dependence on God and space to reimagine possibilities for our lives. I botched that political theory exam. Yet, that letdown became a moment of reimagination. I decided not to give up on my desire to study political theory, particularly with that professor. I visited his office hours, struggled through his class, and did well at the end of the semester. That same professor would become my thesis advisor and mentor. The gift of that failure was the ability to recognize my own limitations and the need for wisdom from others.

Failure as a Gift

It can be challenging to imagine failure as a gift. An F on a paper is not necessarily a gift from someone. Failed friendships or being turned down for a job or internship don't appear to be moments of wisdom and light. When we are moving along in life, failure is a pause for honest self-assessment. In seminary, my senior minister assigned me the role of leading the collegiate ministry of my church in Atlanta with students from Georgia State University, Agnes Scott College, Morehouse College, Spelman College, and Emory University. I was excited to begin this new project; I was full of ideas from my seminary classes about what the church could do to reach college students. With passion and energy, I tried to get things off the ground that first semester. With twenty students, we launched weekly Bible studies, coffee hangouts on each campus, and programming at the church. However, by the end of the semester I was exhausted and only two students showed up to my Bible study. One day one of the two looked at me and said, "Listen, Brandon, this isn't working. (Ouch!) There are only two of us left, out of twenty. Why don't we do what you've been teaching in Bible study and listen to God? Let's scrap this and start fresh; we'll interview students on campus and ask them what they want from this group rather than us pushing a model that doesn't work." At that moment I realized that I failed. I tried to implement ideas that frankly no one else was interested in. The reality of a group of twenty students becoming only two didn't look great when I had to submit a report to my director and the senior minister of our church. Though I was disappointed and initially filled with shame that I had messed up so badly, it was a gift in disguise. Falling short at that moment enabled me to learn some valuable lessons. I was only one person and I needed the insight of a community to launch a successful program. I needed the ability to reimagine what this group could become with the ideas and insights of my students' leadership and not just mine.

Failure is a moment of honest examination of our lives. We are reminded that we are not defined only by our accomplishments or accolades, but in our belovedness. We are participants in a grand narrative that sweeps through history. It is a story of human limitation and God's love that embraces us, claims us, and marks us as God's own beloved children. Our failure is not the definition of who we are. There is more to our lives.

The Grace to Succeed and Fail

As usual, I arrived at my office a few minutes late. Waiting at my door was one of my students. I wondered what she was doing there so early in the morning. "It's about time you got here, Rev. B. I can't wait to tell you all about my failure." I hadn't even had my first cup of coffee for the day, and a student was waiting to tell me how they failed. She rushed into my office, excitedly, plopping down in the office chair. She breathlessly told her story. She reminded me that earlier that semester, I encouraged her to apply for a prestigious fellowship that would enable her to study politics and religion. Without a doubt, we both believed that she would be accepted into this program. However, the day before she received a letter sharing that she had been rejected, and yet as she sat in my office, she was smiling. "I realized in that rejection letter that I was only applying for this fellowship to chase another accomplishment. I have come to realize this isn't what I want to do with my life, that other possibilities might be out there for me." What my student encountered at that moment was the grace of both our failures and successes. In that moment of rejection, a door unexpectedly opened within her to ask herself who she wanted to be.

Grace, as defined by Merriam-Webster, is unmerited divine assistance given to humans for their regeneration or sanctification.[7] Grace is such a lofty theological term, and we think we know it because we can recognize that old hymn *Amazing Grace* quite easily. I like to think of grace as a divine surprise, the unexpected miracle of love, of mercy, of kindness shown to us. There is a grace to our triumphs and disap-

---

7. *Merriam-Webster*, s.v. "grace," accessed August 9, 2019, https://www.merriam
-webster.com/dictionary/grace.

pointments; it is the ability to be surprised by life. We experience this when we accomplish a new task set out before us. We are astounded by grace and our ability to achieve that which we could not imagine. In our failures, we are amazed by beauty in that there are new opportunities, a chance to regroup and find within ourselves a strength we did not know. There is within this blessing the ability to start fresh, to try a new friendship, to change majors or switch colleges, or take on challenges we couldn't imagine trying. Grace is a funny word, hard to explain, but we know how it feels. Our success and our failures are held before us by God's Grace. Frederick Buechner writes:

> Grace is something you can never get, but only be given. . . . The Grace of God means something like: "Here is your life. You might never have been, but you *are*, because the party wouldn't have been complete without you. Here is the world. Beautiful and terrible things will happen. Don't be afraid. I am with you."[8]

Grace is the glue that holds this mystery of our lives together. We cling neither too tightly or too loosely to our lives. With grace, we live with humility and gratitude that we are loved and known. We are still on a journey. Each success and failure is only a piece of your narrative.

College is many things: stressful, exciting, a mystery, a place of becoming and growing. So in the years ahead, don't be afraid to take risks when accomplishing your goals. Do not lead with fear, but work with humility and trust in grace, knowing that you belong to God.

The Prayer of General Thanksgiving from the Book of Common Prayer reminds us of this:

> We thank you for setting us at tasks which demand our best efforts, and for leading us to accomplishments which satisfy and delight us.
> We thank you also for those disappointments and failures that lead us to acknowledge our dependence on you alone.[9]

---

8. Frederick Buechner, "Grace," Frederick Buechner, last modified September 9, 2016, www.frederickbuechner.com/quote-of-the-day/2016/9/9/grace
9. The Book of Common Prayer, 836.

As a seminary professor once said to me, "Work hard, accomplish much, and fail well." You will fail. You will succeed. Live with gratitude and humility, knowing that in every success and every failure, you belong to God.

Going Deeper The path of life is not a clear journey. It is filled with success and failure, but I hope this chapter reminds you that no matter what, you belong to God. Below are some resources that I found helpful in college and in life regarding success and failure.

1. Peter J. Gomes's *The Good Life: Truths That Last in Times of Need* (HarperCollins, 2002).

2. Howard Thurman's *Meditations of the Heart* (Beacon Press, 1999).

3. Henri J. M. Nouwen's *In the Name of Jesus: Reflections on Christian Leadership* (Crossroad, 1992).

4. Peter J. Gomes's 2008 Baccalaureate sermon entitled, "The Virtue of Failure" at Stanford University: https://news.stanford. edu/news/2008/june18/videos/345.html.

5. Check out your office of religious life, find your denomination's chaplain, or a local church affiliated with your denomination. These were the people that reminded me weekly of my belovedness.

CHAPTER 4

RELATIONSHIPS

Olivia Lane

He sat on the couch in my office looking dazed and gazing listlessly at his hands. Four months before, he'd arrived on campus, fresh from the south side of Chicago, hardly believing he was at this incredible university. Finally, his life would be unfolding here among people he never imagined he would call classmates, and after years and years of dreaming, he was on the verge of starting his new reality. But the person who sat across from me now seemed like a shell of the grinning freshman I'd met at the beginning of the semester. We started talking about his experiences on campus; he shared that outside of going to class, he spent most of his time in his room, scrolling through Instagram.

Life at this school was tough, he confessed. He thought because he'd made it this far, he would fit right in, find friends, build his new home away from home. But students were not very welcoming, and he constantly felt caught between two worlds. At home in Chicago, he was the smart kid who made it to the "big time," but at the university, he was "rough around the edges," an outsider who mostly felt like he didn't belong. He was doing well in classes, but he told me that he thought he'd made a mistake, maybe coming here was too much of a reach after all. He didn't want to be a part of something that he wasn't really a part of, and he was tired of trying to imagine this setting could offer him some form of community or belonging.

I started by asking him: "Who are you?" He looked at me with feigned annoyance and stated his name. "But what makes you *you*?" He began to talk at length about the kind of person he was, things that interested him, relationships that were important to him, and suddenly he stopped and looked straight at me with a slightly bewildered look on his face: "I had forgotten who I am . . . like I'm more than one thing and there is a lot that makes me . . . me."

This is true for all of us. Each one of us is unique and complex, and how we extend our personhood into the world is unique and complex. When we remember who we are: complicated and multidimensional people, not defined by any one thing, but enriched by the different strands of our story, and above all, not a mistake, we can be thankful. And when we remember who we are and can express gratitude for who we are, we come to realize that how we exist really does matter.

Relationships

"What do you want to be when you grow up?" The questioning starts early. The question seems harmless enough at three, or again six, but it lingers. It asks us to figure it all out, to have a plan, to make our identity the work that we do, to be the thing that we have declared.

"Where are you going to college?" and then "What is your major?" The questions change slightly, but the intent is the same. Give me the answers about what it is you want to do, and I will determine your place, your value, and your worth. Of course, we are allowed to change our minds; most of us are not pursuing the answers we supplied at three (although our world could use a solid influx of superheroes). And yet, these questions hold real power. Not being able to answer them gives rise to anxiety, frustration, and a feeling that everyone except you has got their life figured out.

When we think about relationships, who we are, and how we relate to the world around us, I want to change the conversation. With an understanding that what we are is already determined by our faith, that identity is already set and established, and that the real question we should be asking one another is, "Who are you, and to whom do you belong?"

Who Are You?

We are not a series of "whats" of careers or public performances—we are souls and bodies that are incredibly complex, and we need to remember that, both for the sake of others and for ourselves.

I cannot talk to you about what we do and why that matters without talking to you about relationships. When I talk about relationships, I always start from the premise that we are relational beings, created by a coeternal triune God, whose essence is threeness, whose identity is relationship and relational. We are created in the image of this relational God and we are designed to be in communion and community with other human beings.

An easier way to say this is that I believe we were created by a God who is for us, and wants us to be for each other and for the world. To truly engage with the idea that God is for us, that God created us good and wants good things for us, means that we have to acknowledge that this is a mandate for humankind, it changes not only how we view ourselves, but how we view all of humanity.

How we embrace a theology of relationship changes how we construct the fabric of connection throughout our lives. *If I believe that I belong to God, and you belong to God, we are part of the same thread. In a sense we belong to each other, and we belong to a story that is larger than our here and now.* It is a story that stretches back through our ancestors and on through our relationships. It is a story that is often colored by brokenness—brokenness that we participate in or which is perpetrated against us—but we know that this story has a triumphant epilogue because it has already been written. Grace and redemption are central themes within the Christian tradition because we need reminders that humans screw up.

The mistakes that we have made, and continue to make, are not the sum of our human experience. We have the opportunity to correct those mistakes, to learn from them, and to change our way of being as a result. Making mistakes (and subsequently correcting and learning from them) is vital to the relational process. As Presbyterian minister and our favorite neighbor Fred Rogers says:

> Mutually caring relationships require kindness and patience, tolerance, optimism, joy in the other's achievements, confidence in oneself, and the ability to give without undue thought of gain. We need to accept the fact that it's not in the power of any human being to

provide all these things all the time. For any of us, mutually caring relationships will always include some measure of unkindness and impatience, intolerance, pessimism, envy, self-doubt, and disappointment.[1]

I don't believe there is a formula for perfect relationships because I don't believe in perfect relationships. Like Mr. Rogers, I believe that our relationships will always include some measure of failure. But that is not the end of the story.

Our culture values perfection very highly. (You can probably easily call to mind messaging you've received about your appearance, grades, career, and happiness.) This emphasis on perfection can make it difficult to recover from a public failure, and there is not always a path of reconciliation. Not only does this lead to "performance"-centered lives, but in certain contexts this makes it impossible to admit an error, even a minor one, because the costs of being wrong are too high. We must be error-free to deserve a place in society.

This mentality bleeds into our relationship with God—we begin to believe that God only loves us when we are doing the right things. We justify things we know to be wrong in our hearts or put off prayer, communion, or fellowship with others until we are regularly "error-free." We think we must be somehow *deserving* of God's love before we dare ask for relationship. But that misses the point of our reconciling God, a God who *first* loved us while we were still sinners. And with God there is always a path of reconciliation. There is no bridge too far. There is no failure that is greater than God's love and forgiveness.

The story of our lives does *not* include our perfection making us worthy of love and relationship, but rather begins with us being loved with a love that holds us in the midst of our proudest moments, and in the midst of our worst. If there is anything I want you to take away from this chapter, it is that *God is for us.* All of us. That is the basis of our story of relationship, and that informs the freedom with which we approach and

---

1. Fred Rogers, *The World According to Mister Rogers: Important Things to Remember* (New York: MJF Books, 2003), 78.

understand others. God is for others too. We are beings who are loved wildly, by the creator of the universe, who redeemed us in this wild story of salvation. When we begin our sense of identity, and our understanding of relationships, by acknowledging that we are all loved, we change the conversation from *what we will be* to *who we will live our lives for.*

Whose Are You?

"God is for us" is a bold theological statement about the basis of our story of relationship with God. This is a story that has its roots in our language of God, especially in the way we speak of the Trinity and the Incarnation. When we say God is Trinity, that communicates a certain relational nature to God from the start. There are three identities bound up in oneness, a concept that is less about us wrapping our minds around logistics, and more about recognizing the way that God participates with God's self and invites us to participate in this relationship with God, through Jesus Christ and the Holy Spirit.

Similarly, an understanding of the Incarnation, the act of God made manifest (born in a human body on earth) in the person of Jesus Christ, shows just how important this image of relationship is to God:

> Let the same mind be in you that was in Christ Jesus, who, though he was in the form of God, did not regard equality with God as something to be exploited, but emptied himself, taking the form of a slave, being born in human likeness. And being found in human form, he humbled himself and became obedient to the point of death—even death on a cross. (Phil. 2:5–8)

The Incarnation shows us a God who intentionally gave up power and entered into a vulnerable position for the sake of knowing and being known to humanity. God desires relationship, and the unified story of the Bible is that we are continually drawn into relationship with God and with one another, and when we break and destroy relationships, God extends grace and restores that which is broken so that we might once again know and be known.

So much of college is about developing expertise: learning and acquiring skills that allow you to be legitimized in your future career. This tends to place a good deal of taxation on our mental well-being, as the parameter for our future success is gauged in a series of papers and exams that indicate how well we test. Here is the thing that college does not often emphasize: not too long after you graduate (probably shortly after you land your first full-time job), people will almost entirely cease to care about the grade you made in an individual class. What will remain important as you journey through life is your ability to pursue, cultivate, and deepen relationships. *Who* you are will always be a factor to the "what" that you are practicing. This "who" piece is what we call formation, or the ongoing process by which we fully experience our human existence.

Here is the thing I know to be true about formation: formation happens all the time. We are constantly being formed whether intentionally or passively, and that formation over weeks and months and years changes our brains, our decision-making processes, who we choose to spend time with, and the things we give ourselves to for work and life. How many hours we spend interacting with social media, how often we are in contact with people who may or may not have the same abilities we have, the same socioeconomic status we have, the same desire or access or religion . . . all of this plays a factor in the person we are becoming and will become.

Proverbs 13:20 says: "Whoever walks with the wise becomes wise, but the companion of fools suffers harm." When you think about who you belong to, this is a multilayered equation. Yes, this encompasses your relationship with God, the time you actually spend investing in your spiritual health, and your understanding of how that impacts your decision-making in the world, but this is also reflected in the people with whom you choose to spend the majority of your hours.

I have noted that choosing wisely and investing in healthy relationships is a critical component of student well-being and growth during the college years. Students who are connected to like-minded community, who have people that they trust across a variety of situations (class, work, religious life, sports teams, etc.), and who are intentional about their closest relationships are more resilient. These students consistently navigate the ups and downs—and there will be ups and downs—of the experience of higher education and have better visioning and perspective when they face challenges.

There are many competing influences for your formation. The noise of college does nothing to help you slow down or put you in a head space where you can identify what is shaping you on a daily basis. The pace at which we live is not always healthy, and frequently not sustainable, so when students are looking to go deeper into questions of belonging, questions largely centered around their understanding of God and how they are or can be in intentional relationship with the cosmic mystery, I encourage them to start with contemplation. I point them toward scripture as an incredible tool for building imagination and understanding of the potential we have as followers of Jesus Christ. Contemplation is a term often used in religious settings to convey staring at or dwelling on something for an extended period of time. This is used in different religious traditions in various ways, but at its core it involves a willingness to sit with texts, ideas, or questions about God.

Ultimately, as you consider what it means to be a beloved follower of Jesus Christ, the questions of relationship, formation, and belonging become valuable not because they are inherently good, but because they are fundamental to our understanding of God, from whom we issue and to whom we return. Our Triune God is relationship in itself: threeness in one, community, giving and loving in action, and invitation. We too are invited into this mystery through faith and called to enact it through our relationships in the world.

How to Apply Relational Thinking

When talking about the practical application of relational thinking, this *who* and *whose* we are, I find the idea of spheres to be useful. Most of our relationships operate in general spheres, and college is one of the first times that those spheres are capable of staying largely separate (see figure 1). Our family life continues to exist largely outside our classroom/college life, which can be fairly separate from our intimate or romantic relationships, all of which can be separate from our religious practice.

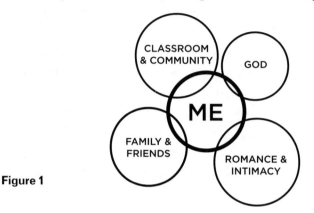

Figure 1

One of the benefits of thinking of relationships in spheres is that it provides mental boundaries for categorizing and prioritizing the time and energy we give to these different spheres. However, thinking of relationships in terms of spheres can also leave us feeling like we have to juggle or balance all our different relationships at once. For the purpose of application, I would like to offer a slightly different way of envisioning relationship spheres to support "The Who" and "Whose" we are exploring (see figure 2).

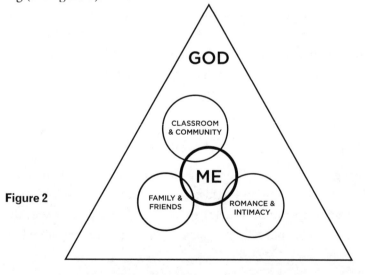

Figure 2

By locating ourselves and all our relationships within a grounding that God holds us, we are relaxed from the need to juggle or sustain things when they become too heavy to hold. For example, you might have a family situation that causes additional stress during your time at college. Maybe you have a sibling that is fighting a lot with your parents, or the health of a loved one is particularly poor, or maybe you even experience the loss of a loved one. Often, students feel overwhelmed and guilty trying to figure out how they should be caring for their family while simultaneously fulfilling their obligations at school. Now, let's assume that keeping the relationships running within all these spheres is not actually your job, but consider instead that it is a gift that you have these relationships, that they are all known to God, and that God is in fact holding them, not you. Perhaps something gets overwhelming with a friendship back home and you begin to feel the spiral of guilt that you cannot be present or available in the ways you might like to be present. If we understand that God is in control, it is perfectly acceptable to allow God to hold those relationships when we are unable to do so. What then becomes a model for building and sustaining healthy relationships in college?

When Jesus was teaching his disciples, one of them asked what was the most important command for their lives, Jesus said: "'You shall love the Lord your God with all your heart, and with all your soul, and with all your mind.' This is the greatest and first commandment. And a second is like it: 'You shall love your neighbor as yourself'" (Matt. 22:37–39). Your fellow students are your neighbors, but your neighbors are not just your fellow students: they are your professors, the administrators, the person who cleans your dorm, the one who serves you meals. Your neighbors are the people who are similar to you and those who are not. How you treat individuals around you, how you develop relationship, matters to your formation and to your practice of faith. In every relationship there is a power dynamic, and it matters deeply how we treat those who are vulnerable, or lack resources, or are just different from us.

Jesus instructed his disciples in Matthew 25, saying whenever they do things for the least of these, for the vulnerable, they do so to Jesus himself. Loving our neighbor becomes a form of right relationship—we engage not because we get anything from another person, but because we believe their story of belonging in Christ Jesus. They are our neighbor and we are called to love them.

"You Don't Need Everyone to Be Your Best Friend!"

The season of college/university occupies such an interesting role in our contemporary context. It is truly an incubator for all kinds of meaningful relationships (mentorship with professors and administrators, spiritual growth and exploration, affinity groups around sports, volunteering, or any number of diverse interests and activities) to blossom. This leads to two common student experiences. The first is that you completely over-book yourself, constantly running from one activity to the next, participating in everything, but consequently not having the time or energy to invest deeply in any single one of those things. Overextending like this leads to high rates of dissatisfaction and burnout. Students can often maintain the schedule for a semester or a year or two, but find themselves "retreating" at some point for the sake of their physical and mental well-being. The second common experience is a sort of delayed fear of missing out, where you figure out your networks early on and begin investing in relationships, only to learn about other "more impressive" or "more interesting" things that peers are doing. You suddenly wonder if you've taken the wrong path or chosen the wrong people to invest in relationally.

Both scenarios are more-or-less mitigated when students are well-grounded in their sense of identity and belonging—this *who* and *whose* understanding. As you think about your spheres of relationship, consider which spheres are easy to hold and which spheres you might need to consider letting God hold for a while. A season of evaluation is always valuable, especially when relationships are especially challenging or draining.

Perhaps a more accurate diagram would be one that depicts the primary, secondary, and tertiary place of various types of relationships in all of our lives. Figuring out what place various relationships and types of relationships occupy in your life can be a great way to discover who is doing your primary formation and how belonging or purpose function because of those relationships. Not all relationships are created equal, and figuring out how to love, value, and live peacefully with other humans in the world takes time and energy to do well.

Being intentional in relationship is key for growth. The following are a couple of questions to ask yourself about how relationships function in your life, how you would like them to function, and what ways you could increase priority or decrease priority based on the positive or negative impact they have on your personhood (creative, emotional, mental, spiritual, and physical).

God

How we think about God, who God is, and what God wants for us and for the world profoundly impacts the way that we engage in relationships for our lives. I wasn't raised in a tradition that encouraged me to imagine God is love, or that God wanted to have a relationship with me. Recognizing God's deep love for the world as inclusive on a broad and personal scale helped transform not only my own experience of relationship with God, but also how I saw others in relation to God. Examine your understanding of God. Does what you know of God broaden your sense of meaning, or does it limit it? What are ways you can engage contemplation on God and relationship as you seek to deepen your spiritual formation?

Family/Friends

Familial relationships and close platonic friendships are going to be a lot of different things during your life. They are almost always in flux and will have different seasons based on temperament, family systems, stage of life, etc. As with any healthy relationship, examine your forms of communication, understand how respect and physical autonomy function and change as you differentiate from your family and forge your own experience of the world. Are you building a new family in college?

Are the people you spend the majority of your time with people who encourage you to deepen your relationships with God and others, or people who isolate you and keep your energy and attention for themselves? The relationships formed during the next four years of your life have the potential to be lifelong; asking yourself if this person reminds you of who you are and whose you are can be helpful in determining if you actually want it to be a lifelong friendship.

Romance/Intimacy

Respect, respect, respect. Thanks for coming to my TED talk. But seriously, respect yourself, ask yourself what it is that you need to be well and whole and do not compromise your sense of self. Express your needs, invite your partner to express their needs, then listen, and if there comes a time when you cannot respect their needs or they cannot respect yours, consider that an intimate relationship may not be a healthy possibility with this individual. At the same time, when building intimate or romantic relationships, be present to the other, ask questions that show intentional listening, and remember details. Showing intentionality in relationship conveys a deep level of care and communicates the significance that individual occupies in your life and formation.

Classroom/Community

Listen for the voice of others. You may think it is easy to identify the most valuable voice in a given situation, but a biblical framework for relationship reminds us that all voices have value because their bearers all have value. Adopt a posture of serving in community, of listening in the classroom, of noticing who takes up space and who does not. If you struggle with finding belonging—and especially if you do not—be an individual who invites others into belonging. Create small groups of people who can share a common interest, check in on a regular basis, be together in person without the use of technology, and share life together. In this way you fulfill your own need to know and be known, but also extend that invitation to others for mutual flourishing.

The Gift of Others

We are relational beings created from relationship and for relationship, and how we choose to embody that in the world says a lot about what we believe about God and about ourselves. Participating in relationship requires some measure of give and take. It asks for those involved to be vulnerable and to accept the other without pretense or coercion. It invites us to be gracious and extend love and understanding, even when we don't feel loved or understood. It invites us to be hospitable, to welcome the stranger. It also involves putting boundaries in place when there is neither respect nor willingness to honor the value of the other person. The gift of relationship is that it puts us in proximity with people who can know us—people who remind us of who we are and whose we are.

Remember my student? He ended up being known, finding a place to be and to belong.

What started as a conversation in my office turned into weekly visits; he befriended other students who also popped in for quick chats, and he began to use his skills and talents to help others. What seemed too difficult to imagine in those first few months of school slowly coalesced into a rich relational experience of community, of knowing and being known.

Going Deeper Here is an invitation to engage more deeply with your relationships:

Think about your most intimate relationships. Do they involve you spending some amount of time just "being" with the other person? This is a central piece of deepening relationship not because it produces a result, but rather because through the process you become familiar, comfortable, and known.

As you consider your identity, how your connection to God operates, and how your connection to other people functions, I would encourage contemplation on the following scripture texts. Pray through them, journal them, ask questions about how they might function in various types of relationships in your life, and what interpretations might be helpful or harmful in different scenarios. This is the beginning of developing a complex ethic and understanding of Christian relationship and how that changes our responsibility both to ourselves and to the world.

John 15:13: "No one has greater love than this, to lay down one's life for one's friends."

Hebrews 10:24–25: "And let us consider how to provoke one another to love and good deeds, not neglecting to meet together, as is the habit of some, but encouraging one another, and all the more as you see the Day approaching."

1 Peter 4:8: "Above all, maintain constant love for one another, for love covers a multitude of sins."

Ephesians 4:1–3: "Lead a life worthy of the calling to which you have been called, with all humility and gentleness, with patience, bearing with one another in love, making every effort to maintain the unity of the Spirit in the bond of peace."

Ephesians 4:32: "And be kind to one another, tenderhearted, forgiving one another, as God in Christ has forgiven you."

CHAPTER 5

WORSHIP

Jonathan Melton

This chapter is about love. And love is like yogurt. Let me explain.

It is not at all uncommon at the University of Wisconsin-Madison to come across students who make their own yogurt, who also want to see you make your own. (Thrift is a virtue among students that the rest of us would do well to emulate.) It's sweet, the determined enthusiasm of the yogurt enthusiasts. To make your own yogurt, you need milk and jars and, well, yogurt. This is where they always lose me. You need yogurt to make yogurt? If I had yogurt, why would I want to make yogurt? But the yogurt you need is the starter, not the whole thing. In the first letter of John, John celebrates God's love as the yogurt that needs no starter, the source of the love to which all other subsequent loves belong, from which all other yogurt comes: "Beloved," he writes, "let us love one another, because love is from God. . . . God's love was revealed among us in this way: God sent his only Son into the world so that we might live through him" (1 John 4:7a, 9). That love, like a starter yogurt strain, claims all the love that ever after comes from it; indeed the starter is active and present in each subsequent batch. And so, your love is a victory not its own.

If asked, most of us can imagine the faces of specific people who have given us the gift of love; these are the people who have shaped our imaginations for what it is to love. Perhaps there was something about the word someone who loved you spoke to you or the hand they extended to you, or the silence a loved one shared with you communicated something of love that you received as a revelation of love. And as such, every act of love we might manage bears an incredible debt to these loves it collects, to the love we received before we shared love. The same is true of those who showed us love. They didn't make it up either; love came to them too. Like the living, active strain found in yogurt, love comes to people and moves through them. We touch, receive, and share in love, and so love is never our possession, but only *participation*. We are always holding love that comes to us from somewhere else. Love has a source.

In a commencement speech, that great theologian of the church Stephen Colbert said to a lawn full of college graduates, "You cannot win your life."[1] It's the kind of thing that sounds true and sensible enough until some jerk cuts you off in traffic. Or you find yourself making a sacrifice that you know no one else will see. You cannot win your life. If life is a victory not its own, then what is true of life is also true of love. You cannot win your love. There's no doing love best, and certainly no doing love better than your partner or your parents or the privileged or the poor. Every victory of your love is a victory for all the loves that came before it and every love that follows it. Every victory of love is for the others. It's true that love wins, but the victory of love comes not from vanquishing enemies, but in celebration and remembrance of the source; in connection to and thanksgiving for the source.

Connection to the source, of course, is exactly what worship is. Worship, therefore, is central and essential to all of our subsequent attempts to communicate love to other people in this world. Activists and public personas throughout the long history of the church like Dorothy Day, Mother Theresa, Martin Luther King Jr., Desmond Tutu, Dietrich Bonhoeffer, and Jean Vanier have all found the grounding for their public work in prayer. It is in prayer that, meeting love's source, we find the freedom to love without fear of even the difficult things about ourselves we will discover as we try to love one another. This freedom begins in the Sunday (or weekday) gathering that ends with the Spirit sending God's People out into the world to encounter each other, to seek and serve Christ in each person, and to practice the good work of trusting that the God who showed up for worship will unfailingly show up there too.

---

1. Stephen Colbert. "Colbert's Commencement Address," Northwestern Newscenter, June 17, 2011, www.northwestern.edu/newscenter/stories/2011/06/colbert-speech-text.html.

I don't know why you participate in worship or don't participate in worship. All I can do is tell you why I choose to make prayer and worship a central part of my life. It has to do with that love that passes from person to person, whose source is Love. What I'd like to do in these few pages is reflect on a few of the things that a life of worship and holy friendship has shown me about the heart and delight of God. Of course, you have been given glimpses of God's heart and delight too, different from mine, and I am convinced there is life for us all (and the world) as we offer our glimpses as gifts to each other. And, of course, here is the crucial claim that is the center of this book: *you are* a part of the heart and delight of God. God takes great joy in you. What's more, as you and I live into God's love together and with all the others, God's joy is made complete.

The Turn and Discovery

One of my favorite things that happens every time Christians get together to discern God's presence "in the practice of receiving a bit of bread and squashed grapes" is where we read from one of the four Gospels, the books of the Bible that contain the Good News about Jesus's life, death, and resurrection.[2] Unlike the other things read before or after it, which might happen somewhere at the front of the church, the Gospel reading customarily takes place in the middle of the people. Maybe the Gospel reader ambles forward in an informal way, or there might be a fancy procession with torches and smoke. The church I currently attend weaves the sacred Gospels through the people with singing and a brightly colored parasol, carried by a child, as people reach out to touch the book or bow as it moves by. The important thing is that before it is read the life, death, and resurrection of Jesus now stands at the center of the gathering's common life.

As the Gospel book makes its way to the center of the people, the people usually turn toward the book, following the movement, and their movement changes the energy of the worship. Without the turning, the

---

2. Amy Laura Hall, *Laughing at the Devil: Seeing the World with Julian of Norwich* (Durham, NC: Duke University Press, 2018), 3.

book is merely descriptively at the center of things, but the turning turns the individuals who showed up that day into a people centered on Jesus.

What I especially love about the turning is the unique instruction that makes the turning possible. In fact, there's only one way to tell people to move that really works. It doesn't work, for example, to say, "Everybody turn to the left!" or "Quarter-turn to the right!" That instruction would work for some people, the same way a broken clock is correct two times a day, but others would hit their noses on the wall. No, the only instruction that universally works for the moment is to say, "However you find yourself, turn and face the Good News of the life, death, and resurrection of Jesus." As everybody does this, the community becomes centered on Jesus. So the practical "ask" of the instruction is entirely unique to each individual. Some will turn a little, some a lot, and others not at all. Young children might find it necessary to stand on top of pews or move closer. The call requires personal interpretation; the only person who intimately knows what is asked of you in that moment is you.

And yet. The instruction is not *only* personal; after all, the call is not to center yourself on the gospel. The instruction is to turn in whatever way puts the gospel before you and subsequently makes the gospel the center of the community's life. Turn to see the Good News of Jesus, discover yourself as a part of the body of Christ. This is the miracle of being re-membered as God's People. If this isn't exactly why we go to church, it is at least how we come to discover ourselves as a church once we show up. We go to remember and, to our great surprise, discover that re-membering begins with God, who is unendingly gathering all things to God's self, even us.

Being Re-Membered

To receive God's re-membering of us as a gift requires two things, I think. The first thing it requires is that we come to see and speak honestly about the many ways the world atomizes us into mere individuals. That is, we must come to mistrust the mistrust we are often told (and trained) to have toward one another. It's the irony of extreme individualism: that it's a story that others tell (and sell) us.

To be blunt, there are lots of entities with lots of money and lots of incentive to structure a world in which individuals and groups of individuals fear one another. For-profit corporations, for example, recognize that when neighbors cannot trust one another, and subsequently do not share goods that might otherwise be held in common (like lawn mowers) with one another, people buy more stuff. It is shocking to consider how much of what we buy "because I want one" also shares a sibling motivation: because we do not know (or trust) our neighbors.

Some days we might be afraid of being harmed, but maybe other days we're simply afraid that the others will impede us from becoming our "best selves." Either fear serves the purpose of isolation and preys upon the conviction that you are not enough, that your flourishing is found in separating yourself from those God has given us as neighbors and friends who, belonging to God, also belong to each other. The training of individualism runs so deep that we can almost universally assume ourselves to be proficient in this malformation, and in ways we cannot see by ourselves.

The second thing that is necessary to receive God's re-membering of us as a gift, then, comes out of the first, and it is to dare to believe that this atomizing is a loss to us, even as individuals, and to our efforts to know the love of God.

Without reckoning with the reality of this fragmentation and isolation, we will miss the radical gift of Christian worship, *even if we go to church.* Left to the default of the world's imagination, whatever we do or don't do on Sundays in a building called church will be less than it could be; worship will be reduced to an exercise of individual piety enacted in the presence of others similarly engaging individual piety for the sake of becoming better individual people (not unlike the way small children practice parallel play—the children look for all the world like they're playing together, but in truth they are playing by themselves, alone, side by side).

But the life of faith is for making us truer people, not better individuals. The task is confession, not self-improvement. And the truth we will learn to tell begins with the grounding word that we belong to God and one another, and that God's love for us is the most true thing about us.

Prayer and the Early Church

I find it helpful (and comforting) to see how the work of discovering one-self in the context of the community of faith has been a challenge for followers of Jesus from the very beginning. When Paul, for example, warned the church in Corinth that "all who eat and drink without discerning the body, eat and drink judgment against themselves" (1 Cor. 11:29), it is clear from the surrounding verses that Paul is speaking to Christians who come to the Lord's Supper oblivious to and without regard for each other. Maybe the Christians in Corinth, from a malicious posture, did not care that some at the table didn't have food, even as they drank too much, but maybe too they simply did not see the others. And which is worse?

One time I asked a group of students after worship if they felt like a life lived in the Episcopal Church would equip them to pray for each other, as sisters, brothers, and holy friends, in the weeds of particulars, by name, together. "Jonathan," one student offered, "what about what we do is preparing us for that?" "Well, lots," I thought to myself. But I cherished the student's honesty, which prompted a follow-up question, "Is that something you want to be able to ask for and give one another?" Her answer came quickly, "Yes! What does it look like to come to the table with open hearts for one another?"

We come to the table to see Jesus, to see more of God. However, God does not grant us this vision apart from the rest of humanity to which Jesus belongs. Most of us did not ask for the rest of the people called "church," but church is the gift God gives us anyway. Thank God.

Becoming Yourself

Christians discover, as often as they gather, the God who loves us and the others God loves. We also discover ourselves more truly for our relationship to the rest of the body. As we grow in knowing and being known in the people called church, we discover the truth that *you cannot know yourself by yourself*. This truth is both obvious and radical.

The truth is obvious in its practical dimensions: you can't see the back of your own head without the help of external resources, like mirrors, for example. Whether in athletics, academics, performance, or anything else, the acknowledgment of blind spots and the value of honest feedback has a demonstrable, positive, and causative relationship to flourishing that only the foolish question.

But the truth that you cannot know yourself by yourself also has its more clearly spiritual dimensions: if it is true that we belong to one another because we belong to God, then our gifts find their right ordering and fullest potential as we offer them up to the glory of God and the building up of the People of God. Generosity simultaneously makes self-discovery and belonging possible.

We become more truthful and so more truly ourselves as we live in right relationship with our community and our neighbors. To live more truly is a goal that suggests we each have some pretending to give up. Sometimes we pretend that each of us is a "self-made person," forgetting that "our life depends upon each other's toil."[3] But the self-made person is an illusion that betrays us, because it turns out that getting up each day to engage the work of making ourselves worthy of love is cripplingly lonely. With time, it becomes clear that our pretending covers deep wounds: the struggle of each person to believe that she is worthy of love.

The Love That Makes Us Lovely

In promising ourselves and our gifts to God and others, we will inevitably disappoint our own expectations for the gifts we have promised. This too is a gift: we will be given opportunities to experience love and forgiveness in the face of disappointment. In short, we will be asked to trust and discover that our belovedness does not depend on our doing enough, or anything, to deserve it.

A friend said to me one time, "If I'm honest, I don't *want* unconditional love. I want God to love me because I'm the best one." I doubt most of us would say this thought out loud, but exactly because my friend is not alone in having considered the thought, her saying it for the rest of us is a gift. What other skills, attributes, privileges, identities—beyond

---

3. The Book of Common Prayer, 134.

"beloved child of God"—do we trust for assurance that we matter and can be loved? Who are you underneath all of these things, in that place where "all our strivings cease"?[4]

An author and friend one time inquired of a priest what she might give up for Lent.[5] "I don't find much meaning in giving up things like desserts or cigarettes," she confessed. The priest thought for a moment. "Well," she began, "Lent gives us an opportunity to trust our belovedness and so to put down everything we might be tempted to trust as the most important thing about us. We don't give up bad things so much as trust-more-than-God things. You are a writer. I wonder if you would consider giving up reading for Lent?" The priest's suggestions hint at what it must mean to become more truly ourselves as we discover ourselves with God and one another, as we grow to trust the truth of God's love in that space. God's love for you is the most important thing about you.

Confession: like my friends, I sometimes find it difficult to let go of the desire to impress God. "I know, I know, God already loves me, but won't God appreciate how I showed love to this one? I mean, to put up with that creep! I know *I'm* impressed." Even when I'm less confident, I nevertheless sometimes imagine my love, per our earlier conversation, as an individual action, for which success or failure is equally mine to claim. But then I remember that none of us came up with love by ourselves. Love is a reality made known to us through others. So each encounter with even our own impressive-to-us love for others is a participation in a mysterious gift. Love is always a beautiful, bewildering gift.

Practicing Silence, Learning to Speak

All four of the Gospels recount that when the soldiers, chief priests, and elders find Jesus and his friends in the Garden of Gethsemane, setting in motion the series of events that will lead to Jesus's death, the instinct of

---

4. "Dear God and Father of Mankind," *The Hymnal 1982* (New York: Church Hymnal, 1982), hymn 653.

5. Lent is the forty-day season of prayer and penitence before we celebrate Holy Week and Easter.

Jesus's followers is to fight for him and, probably not incidentally, also for themselves (Matt. 26, Mark 14, Luke 22, John 18). In three of the Gospel accounts, Jesus explicitly tells those who would follow him to put their swords away. Some Christians interpret Jesus's command as extending beyond that moment. That is, Christians learn in this moment that to rightly follow Jesus is to live a Christ-centered commitment to nonviolence. Christians are those who have put away the sword.

Whether or not one understands the nonviolence of Christ to extend to realities like war (not a small or unimportant question), all Christians are invited to consider and take up postures of vulnerability. Christians do not grow nearer to any of the things at the center of our common life through violent defense of God or ourselves.

That's where silence comes in. When Christians gather in an organized way, most of our prayers allow for silence. Oftentimes, though, Christians underutilize this form of prayer. But the reasons silence can be awkward or scary are the same reasons silence is so powerful: silence is the form prayer takes when we put all the weapons away. Whether we were using them to defend God or ourselves matters little. To practice silence is to profess confidence in the One who meets us in that space and to live by what, in that space, God gives us.

Taizé is a place in France and an ecumenical order of brothers who gather to pray three times a day. They observe a sizable silence as a part of each prayer. Several years ago, at an organizing gathering for a Taizé Pilgrimage of Trust, one of the attendees asked one of the brothers of Taizé how the brother used the silences. What did he do in them?

The brother received the question well. "It's a good question!" he said. "Three prayers a day for thirty years for me now. . . . What does one do?" The brother went on to share that what he does is rest in and receive God's love for him. "That's the first thing," he said. "Some days it's the only thing. If I only get as far as that, that is enough."

The brother's simple answer had a moving and radical effect on me. I had practiced contemplative prayer before, mostly looking for a word or short set of words to keep before me, but it almost always felt like trying to get it right. Here, the brother suggested, the effort belonged to God and my work was to begin to trust it. My work was to put down my swords. But since we are trained to make ourselves into people worthy of love and admiration, disarming oneself or one's community is easier said than done. Silence can help.

As I shared earlier, Stephen Colbert once addressed a class of university graduates with the unhappy news that "you cannot win your life." He was borrowing from improv theatre to explain what makes for good improv actors. The first thing, says Colbert, that a good improv player has to surrender is the desire to win the scene.[6] In the absence of a game to win, Colbert suggests that the best players are the most generous ones, the ones with whom it is fun to play, the ones who do not need to be in control.

As I begin to surrender and learn to trust, believing in my bones God's love for me, without any contribution of my own, I become capable of focusing less on myself. I'm playing with house money! Having become a friend of silence, I can speak more truthfully, unguardedly. I can pursue God's righteousness on some days from a position of contrition, that is, as someone who has not always or even frequently been right. I can even *lead* with my weakness and see if Paul was right, that that's where God's strength is known. The most true thing about me does not depend on me. Our lives become living witnesses to the presence and activity of God.

Sing a New Song

When I was in college and involved in campus ministry, I was apprenticed to a priest in my particular role as the Canterbury sacristan. This role involved making some decisions about the prayers, but it mostly involved arriving early to the evening service and preparing the space for the community's weekly Eucharist. The work was not glamorous and the behind the scenes dimensions suited me in that season probably as well as any kind of work could have. I vividly remember moving about the sanctuary, setting the table and marking the books, as the evening

---

6. Google "Michael Scott" and "improv class" for a tremendous example of how not to do improv.

light streamed through the church's stained-glass windows, filling the space with brilliant streaks of color. Many times, though I thought I was alone, I would hear a distant voice singing. It was always the priest. She would be down in the undercroft, checking into her office, also preparing. I don't know if she didn't think she was also alone, but it was also clear to me that being aware of my being there wouldn't have kept her from singing. She sang hymns, and she sang them joyfully and beautifully. Her songs became permission for me to make space in my life for the unfiltered expressions of joy my heart also held.

My prayer is that your experience of worship also ignites expressions of joy and thanksgiving that exceed the container of the occasion that began them. Worship is rhythm: the people gathered and centered, the book in their midst, the prayers, the wine and the bread, the blessing and sending, the going and discerning and collecting and coming again, so that we might lift up our hearts with new bits of creation this time around. The rhythm of the new creation as God makes all creation new.

As I grow in this life of faith, as my attention waxes and wanes and comes back again, as I navigate the ups and downs of remembering and belonging and trust, I notice myself, like my campus ministry priest, singing songs of praise in the in-between spaces especially during those seasons of spiritual flourishing. Not everyone sings, of course, but everyone's heart finds some spontaneously joyful response when seized by the truth of the love that first moved the sun and the stars. What songs has God put in your heart? I want to share a verse from one of the songs I sing most frequently as a prayer with which to end this time together, a picture of the potential for prayer to be transformed by trust in the love of God made known to us in Christ Jesus:

> For the love of God is broader than the measure of the mind;
>   and the heart of the Eternal is most wonderfully kind.
> If our love were but more faithful, we should take him at his word;
>   and our life would be thanksgiving, for the goodness of the Lord.[7]

---

7. "There's a Wideness in God's Mercy," *The Hymnal 1982* (New York: Church Hymnal, 1982), hymn 469, 470.

Going Deeper I realize this chapter on worship and prayer has been scant on practical details of the "how to" variety. (I don't exactly apologize for this.) If there is a list to summarize, the initial three-part summary goes something like this:

1. Don't only (or even primarily) pray alone. When you pray, risk being known in the community of faith.

2. Seek to become truer, not better. Risk finding yourself in stories for which you are not the hero.

3. Let the community of faith help you trust God's love for you. Be a generous giver and receiver of love, which has its source in God.

In case, though, you are among those earnestly looking for some "this is how to do it" stuff, here are a few ideas:

- Make a list of the hymns and scriptures you know by heart. Note, I'm not saying you should start by memorizing anything; just observe what you have memorized. It's okay if the list is short. Notice where your heart lights up as it seeks and explores the presence of God.

- Utilize the written prayers of other people, the living and the dead. Read them and steal them, if you like them. Use the Book of Common Prayer, but don't limit yourself to denominational books of prayer. Read books about and memoirs by holy people you admire. Read for an eye for how they read scripture and the ways scripture shaped their lives and their prayers. Find another person with whom to share these observations.

- Read the psalms and take them up as the invitation they are to be unflinchingly honest in conversation with God.

- Find others to pray with on the days between Sundays.

- Give generously of yourself in and outside of your faith community. Do one thing you're not sure you're up to. Be open to receiving instruction or help.

In addition, here are some great books and resources about prayer:

- Margaret Guenther's *The Practice of Prayer: The Church's Teaching Series, Vol. 4* (Cambridge, MA: Cowley Publications, 1998).

- Jonathan Melton's "Daily Bread: An Annotated Bibliography of Select Online Resources for Daily Prayer," *The Patience of Trees* (blog),July12,2016,http://thepatienceoftrees.blogspot.com/2016/07/daily-bread-annotated-bibliography-of.html.

- C. Christopher Smith and John Pattison's *Slow Church: Cultivating Community in the Patience Way of Jesus* (Downers Grove, IL: InterVarsity Press, 2014).

- Rowan Williams's *Silence and Honey Cakes: The Wisdom of the Desert* (Oxford: Lion Hudson, 2004).

- Jonathan Wilson-Hartgrove's *Reconstructing the Gospel: Finding Freedom from Slaveholder Religion* (Downers Grove, IL: InterVarsity Press, 2018).

CHAPTER 6

GOD MADE THE RAINBOW

Adrienne Koch

When God made the rainbow for the first time, the worst imaginable thing had just happened. God erased the world.[1] The masterful artist who created all things "in the beginning" (Gen. 1:1a) turned the pencil upside-down and blotted out everything drawn on the first few pages of the bible:

> [God erased] every living thing that was on the face of the ground, human beings and animals and creeping things and birds of the air; they were [erased] from the earth. Only Noah was left, and those that were with him in the ark. (Gen. 7:23)

As someone who grew up in the church, I learned the story of Noah's ark at a young age. Noah was a felt board character, a Vacation Bible School cut-out, a crazy old man with a white beard who showed up in skits wearing a big brown boat like a skirt. But Noah was also the harbinger of nightmares. In my childhood dreams, the sky was blood red, spattered with foreboding purple clouds through which an apologetic God cried torrential tears to drown the world.[2]

Sometimes I became Noah in those nightmares—my subconscious's last-ditch effort to stop the dream from killing me. I was left standing, staring out over the dark and watery expanse that was once all I had known. Noah lived that nightmare for about a year, hidden away in a small wooden box—floating in the closet of the world. When Noah

---

1. הְחָמ is the Hebrew/Aramaic word in Genesis 7:23 that can be translated as "erased."

2. Genesis 6:6 indicates that God was grieved "to his heart" for making humankind after realizing they had done so much evil to one another.

finally came out, the prayer that he prayed rose like incense to the nostrils of God. And that's when the rainbow came. God sent a bow in the sky that reached from heaven to earth, and promised never to erase humankind like that again (Gen. 9:11–13).

Thousands of years after God made a rainbow for Noah, Gilbert Baker made a rainbow for Harvey Milk and sold it for $1,000.[3] Today, that symbol is widely understood as the flag of the worldwide LGBTQ+ nation. I don't know if Baker's intention was to connect his rainbow to the rainbow in the Bible, but I do know that Baker intentionally never copyrighted the rainbow flag: "He wanted it to be owned by everyone." [4] That means that Baker's flag is my flag too, and my Christian imagination can't separate the rainbow flag billowing in the wind on the banister of a downtown hair salon from the story of Noah because I am a gay priest. I am both a lover of God and a lover of another woman. Whenever I see a rainbow, I remember God's promise not to destroy me.

That's the fear, isn't it? Whether you're a cradle Christian, a curious agnostic burned by a judgmental religion, or one of the "nones" who avoids walking into any building with a top that resembles a steeple, if you stand proudly under the flag of the LGBTQ+ nation, somewhere along the way you heard the church teach that God erases mistakes like you. Why would you trust that God?

Asking this question still knots my stomach because I first asked it in a puddle of tears on my college dorm room floor twenty years ago. In college, I was sure God would destroy me for falling in love with another woman. But unlike so many of the stories I hear from other gay folk my age, the church was gracious to me. As a young adult in closeted relationships, I expected every Sunday sermon to expose me to the crowds and smite me to hell. Instead, every Sunday I was reminded of God's love for me. I thought being gay meant I was one of the wicked people God wanted to erase from the world, but God treated me like Noah, as a per-

---

3. Curtis M Wong, "This History and Meaning of the Rainbow Pride Flag," huffpost .com, June 7, 2018, www.huffpost.com/entry/rainbow-pride-flag-history_n_5b193aafe4 b0599bc6e124a0.

4. Ibid.

son of faith. I always felt God's love for me, even when I didn't love myself. Sometimes I wonder if God taught me this truth so that I can share it with others like me, whose sexuality and gender is non-normative. That truth is this: *you are not a mistake to be erased.* You are the beloved of God.

And just as Noah was not alone on his boat, I am not the sole Christian minister on this church ship who knows the belovedness of queer folk. I work with Presbyterians and Lutherans, Cooperative Baptists, and Methodists (not to mention a whole crew of queer-loving Jews) who, along with their religious bodies and, at times, in spite of them, have made it their jobs to make sure LGBTQ+ folk know how much we are loved.

I'm writing these words from my office in the Cheshire House, which is the home of Episcopal Campus Ministry in Raleigh, North Carolina, where a group of collegiate and noncollegiate young adults are also working hard to make sure than anyone who does not conform to normative standards of sexual and gender expression know that they have a place in God's community. This group calls themselves "Brave Space."[5] The founders, who identify as LGBTQ+, were inspired by the words of womanist poet Micky ScottBey Jones in "Invitation to Brave Space:"

> Together we will create *brave space*
> Because there is no such thing as a "safe space."[6]

These young adults know the church is not a safe space for queer folk, and they also know that it can be a brave space—so that's what they call themselves. Their name reminds them to be brave. Brave Space is a queer theology discussion group where queer young adults study queer thinkers and theologians and take turns leading topical conversations about God and faith that relate to their everyday lives. Some Christians in the group are learning to be brave about coming out as queer to their families and churches. Others in the group are learning to be brave

---

5. You can read more about Brave Space in the Raleigh Hub Groups section of the yeah NC app, downloadable at https://subsplash.com/yeahNC/app or in your app store.

6. Micky ScottBey Jones, "Invitation to Brave Space," mickyscottbeyjones.com, June 13, 2017, www.mickyscottbeyjones.com/invitation-to-brave-space/.

about coming out as Christian in their queer circles of friends, because, let's be honest, Christianity and "homosexuality" haven't played nice together for a long time.

My experience has taught me that the LGBTQ+ Nation and the Christian Church can become friends. Our best mediator and greatest ally is Jesus. The message in the Gospels and the letters of the early Church is not just "you're not a mistake," but rather, you are and have always been loved by a God who is love incarnate, and who created you to love others: "Beloved, let us love one another, because love is from God; everyone who loves is born of God and knows God. Whoever does not love does not know God, for God is love" (1 John 4:7–8).

An Ally in Jesus

"Where are you and Jesus, right now?" the Rt. Rev. Michael Curry asked me as I sat in his office at the Diocesan House in North Carolina for the first time, aspiring to become a priest in the Episcopal Church.

Bishop Curry was always asking questions about Jesus—in his sermons, over lunch, and in his interviews with would-be priests.[7] So when I became a priest and a spiritual director, it's no surprise that I found myself asking the same question to others that the good bishop asked me.

Not long ago, I sat in my office with Stephen, a university student who grew up in a church that does not believe in "homosexuals," but believes that sexual acts between members of the same biological sex are sinful. Stephen is now a young adult trying to make sense of his first romantic relationship with another man. If we talk about morals and ethics when we meet, the conversation becomes confusing to him. Bible verses are torn out of context and taped back together in a hodge-podge theology that always ends in judgement, condemnation, and self-hatred.

Whenever I ask, "Where are you and Jesus, right now?" something sparks in his eyes, triggering his biblical imagination in such a way that

---

7. If you haven't heard his sermon preached at the royal wedding of Prince Harry and Meghan Markle on May 18, 2018, in Windsor, England, it is all about the love of God in Jesus. You can find it here: www.youtube.com/watch?v=5gonlKodrmk.

the doctrine he grew up with disappears, leaving just one person to reckon with, someone who helps him feel brave—Jesus.

On this particular day, when I asked Stephen the "Bishop-Curry-question," he told me a story from the Gospel of Luke: "I am with Jesus and he is saying to me, 'Follow me,' but I say, 'Lord, first let me go and bury my father.' I put my hand to the plow and I look back."[8]

There is palpable vulnerability in Stephen's response that is not unfamiliar. In my own work leading Bible study on these verses over the years, I've noticed that some people squirm in their seats at Jesus's words. People assume Jesus is angry with the man who asked to go and bury his father, pointing out a hypocritical impulse. But this perspective isn't usually from a close reading of peer-reviewed commentaries. Instead, it's from a cursory glance at the chapter's section heading.

It may surprise you to know, as it has some of my students, that the section headings in English translations of the Bible are not holy writ; they are contemporary summaries offered by book editors. And a common section heading for this portion of scripture is: "Would-be followers of Jesus."

A "would-be," by definition, is simply someone who desires to be like someone else, but the colloquial term for a "would-be" is a "wannabe"—someone who is trying (all too obviously) to fit in, poorly emulating the person they want to be like.

Stephen is worried that being gay means he has lost his chance at being a true follower of Jesus. He's afraid that he's forever relegated to Luke's list of wannabes. But if Jesus is the LGBTQ+ nation's greatest ally in the church, then there has to be more to being a Christian in Stephen's story than his sexuality. In fact, you may have heard it said elsewhere that in the Bible Jesus never talks about same-sex relationships or actions, ever. That's true. So these brief encounters with Jesus have nothing to do with sexuality and everything to do with a different kind of social marker: Jesus's Jewishness. To explore how Jesus is an ally to LGBTQ+ folks, we have to let him self-identify rather than place all of our labels and religious expectations on him. Fair? Whatever your image of Jesus may be on the spectrum of somber crucifix to laughable bobblehead, Jesus is more

---

8. This is derived from Luke 9:58–60.

than an icon—he's a person, a Jewish person, who is called "the Son of God" by others, and in the story Stephen referred to Jesus calling himself "the Son of Man." Let's read that section of Luke for ourselves:

> When the days drew near for [Jesus] to be taken up, he set his face to go to Jerusalem. And he sent messengers ahead of him. On their way they entered a village of the Samaritans to make ready for him; but they did not receive him, because his face was set toward Jerusalem. When his disciples James and John saw it, they said, "Lord, do you want us to command fire to come down from heaven and consume them?" But he turned and rebuked them. Then they went on to another village.
>
> As they were going along the road, someone said to him, "I will follow you wherever you go." And Jesus said to him, "Foxes have holes, and birds of the air have nests; but the Son of Man has nowhere to lay his head." To another he said, "Follow me." But he said, "Lord, first let me go and bury my father." But Jesus said to him, "Let the dead bury their own dead; but as for you, go and proclaim the kingdom of God." Another said, "I will follow you, Lord; but let me first say farewell to those at my home." Jesus said to him, "No one who puts a hand to the plow and looks back is fit for the kingdom of God." (Luke 9:51–62)

Before we get to the "wannabes'" interactions with Jesus, notice the opening story. Jesus hears about a group of "half-Jews" who don't want anything to do with him. Jesus's followers become indignant and ask Jesus if it's okay to bring down a rain of fire from heaven to destroy the Samaritans. I wonder if Jesus saw a rainbow in the sky or in his mind, because he quickly turns to his friends and tells them that destroying people is not the way followers of Jesus handle personal rejection. And the group seems to move on. But what comes next are three encounters about people invited to follow Jesus. As stated, I've encountered people who believe these three interactions are about wannabe followers of Jesus, but when read in context with the previous paragraph, I think Jesus is offering three examples of people who are on the path toward becoming true followers. Maybe that's the path Stephen is on too.

There are a few important facts to name before we dive into the stories behind each encounter. We've already established that Jesus is

Jewish, and it's likely that the people in these interactions are Jewish. All of the biblical authors are Jewish (or of Jewish descent), and in their writings they usually indicate when someone is not Jewish—that doesn't happen here, so these interactions are probably all between Jews, which is why it's important to note that the three sayings of the wannabes are three nearly verbatim quotations from significant people in Jewish history:

> "Wherever you go I will go." Ruth said to Naomi.
> "Let me go and bury my father." Joseph said to Pharaoh.
> "Let me say farewell to those at my home." Elisha said to Elijah.

If we want to know what it means to follow Jesus, we should first ask what it meant for Ruth to follow Naomi, for Joseph to bury his father, and for Elisha to say farewell to his home.

Ruth Follows Naomi

The first person in the Jewish imagination to say "wherever you go, I will go" (Ruth 1:16 NKJV) was Ruth, an immigrant who left her homeland of Moab to remain with her mother-in-law after both women were widowed. Ruth has a biblical book named after her, and it is the only book in the Bible that seems to have no obvious "bad guys." The book begins with terrible things happening to ordinary people; things like racism and poverty and death. But it turns out that all of those dreadful things are the precursor to this part of Ruth's story, which is about a God who heals the relationships of ordinary people through loving-kindness. In Hebrew, the word for loving-kindness is *hesed*. It shows up hundreds of times in the Old Testament and is a major descriptor of God's character and person, "Give thanks to the Lord, for he is good, for his steadfast [*hesed*] endures forever" (Ps. 118:29). Ruth's story reveals God's love for and through ordinary people like you, like me, and like Stephen.

So let's assume that when the supposed wannabe says to Jesus, "I will follow you wherever you go" (Luke 9:57b), Jesus's Jewish memory is triggered to remember Ruth's story. With these words, Ruth committed herself to her Jewish mother-in-law, Naomi, and because of Ruth's faithfulness to a Jew, one of God's chosen people, God committed to care for both women. And God did. By the end of the book of Ruth, these women are squarely situated in a prominent Jewish family and Ruth is on her way to being one of the five women later named in the genealogy of Jesus. In short, the man Jesus encounters just quoted Jesus's great-great-greatish grandmother, and this is Jesus's response: "Foxes have holes, and birds of the air have nests; but the Son of Man has nowhere to lay his head."

Jesus responds to that nod to his grandma by letting the man know that he hears the commitment in his words. Jesus wants to be clear that he's not leading the man to any traditional sense of family and home that he's ever known. Jesus's ministry journey, from the start, has been a redefinition of home. When he taught "in my Father's house there are many dwelling places" (John 14:2a NIV), he was not talking about his earthly father, Joseph of Nazareth, and the family hut back in Bethlehem. Jesus was talking about a home that is non-normative in that it is not yet on this earth. Because his words come on the heels of a quotation from the book of Ruth, it's also clear that the out-of-this-world home of Jesus will be full of God's loving-kindness for Jews like this man, and non-Jews like Ruth. In Jesus's eyes all of us have become his chosen people. He isn't rebuking the man for his heartfelt words of devotion, he's inviting that man and all of us to come home with him.

Joseph Buries His Father

Joseph's story is perhaps one of the greatest coming-out stories in all of scripture. Like many queer folk, Joseph feels most exposed at the thought of coming out to his family. For him, the difficult relationships are with his brothers. They were the cause of the first major trauma in Joseph's life—they sold him into slavery when he was a boy.

Years later, Joseph's brothers experience their own trauma—a famine. In order to save themselves and their family, these brothers travel to Egypt where it's rumored there is food in abundance. What they don't know is that the man who has been placed in charge of food distribution is the brother they sold. If these brothers are going to survive, they will have to face their past in the face of Joseph. The twist in the plot is that when his brothers show up at Joseph's door and he recognizes them, they don't recognize him—this is the coming-out part—Joseph has to decide whether to come out as himself.

After having a little fun with the power inherent in his position and playing a few tricks on his brothers, Joseph finally tells them who he is. Through a lump in his throat and a tear-soaked face, he sets aside his right to vengeance and recounts his story as one full of God's grace. It takes courage to come out as yourself to family, and Joseph manages to do so with kindness.

The way Joseph comes out reminds me that it was so much easier for me to come out as gay in the church once I began meeting other gay Christians. I often liked being around them better than straight folk, not because of sexuality, but because the hardships of life seemed to have chiseled away the sharp edges of their personalities and left them with deep self-understanding and faith in God's goodness. That's what seems to have happened to Joseph. Through the hardships, he managed to become more himself, more comfortable in his own skin and in his own story, and as we'll soon see, in his new home.

Joseph's brothers are not as graceful; they are terrified. They worry what Joseph might do to them. In the end, Joseph doesn't only withhold vengeance, he welcomes his entire family with open arms, inviting them to live with him in Egypt. Joseph can't leave his family to starve when he is lord of riches in Pharaoh's land. So the whole family moves into Joseph's house. It is there, in Egypt, that Joseph's father, Israel (Jacob), dies.

Upon the death of Israel, Joseph makes a bold request of his boss (read: slave-owner), Pharaoh: "Let me go up, so that I may bury my father; then I will return" (Gen. 50:5c). Joseph had promised his father that upon his death Joseph would return Israel's body to the land that God promised the Israelites. Now I don't know if Joseph actually wanted to return to Egypt; he was a slave and may have had little choice in the matter. But Pharaoh had a choice whether to let Joseph go or not, and he let him go, trusting that Joseph would return.

This brings us to the would-be follower of Jesus's words: "Lord, first let me go and bury my father" (Luke 9:59). Let's assume that Jesus's Jewish memory is triggered yet again; after all, Joseph was Jesus's great-

great-greatish uncle. So if Jesus hears Joseph in this man's response to the invitation, "Follow me," then the words, "Let the dead bury their own dead; but as for you, go and proclaim the kingdom of God" (Luke 9:60), take on a very personal meaning.

There are a lot of layers to Jesus's response. It's not just that Joseph is related to him, but also that Joseph's father, Israel, is the father of the Israelites, an entire generation of Jesus's ancestors who were enslaved in Egypt after Joseph died and a new Pharaoh came to power. The Israelites are the ones who were led by Moses to receive the Ten Commandments, the holy Torah of God. Torah is a word that encompasses all of Jewish religious law, the law that Jesus tells his followers he has come to fulfill (Matt. 5:17–20). So when Jesus hears this nod to his uncle Joe, he wants to be clear that being a follower of Jesus has everything to do with burying Israel. Jesus's message, from the beginning, has been about fulfilling the law so that a new community of faith can be ushered in, a new family of God that is open to more than just the people of Israel because the new law isn't written on stone tablets handed to a few, but on human hearts (1 Cor. 3:3) accessible to everyone.

This new family of Jesus will not be established on the law given to Israel. Those laws can be buried by those who died under them. Anyone who wants to follow Jesus will have to walk a new path toward a new community that he calls "the kingdom of God."

Elisha Says Farewell to His Family

The familial themes that show up in the first two encounters continue in the third, which quotes Elisha, a man set up to be the prophet Elijah's successor. When Elijah approaches Elisha to anoint him a prophet, Elisha is in the middle of plowing a field. In response to the invitation, Elisha turns to Elijah and says, "Let me kiss my father and my mother, and then I will follow you" (1 Kings 19:20). Elijah allows the request, implying that it is not he who calls the man to greater purpose, but God. So Elisha returns home and says goodbye to his family with panache. In a grand gesture he burns the wood of his farming plow and uses the metal to slaughter the animals yoked to it. He destroys his previous means of survival and uses it to host a feast for his family and the surrounding community. Then Elisha follows Elijah.

So when a man approaches Jesus and says, "I will follow you, Lord; but let me first say farewell to those at my home" (Luke 9:61), Jesus has got to be excited. The message he has been preaching is finally landing in its hearers' hearts. Jesus doesn't want people to quote his family members to him, he wants them to do what his ancestors did—leave everything and follow where God leads. And I think Jesus also wants to break open this whole awesome Jewish thing and make it for everybody. These stories point to Jew and non-Jew becoming one family. The apostle Paul confirms my suspicion that this is one of Jesus's primary criteria for membership in the kingdom of God, when he writes in Galatians 3:28: "There is no longer Jew or Greek, there is no longer slave or free, there is no longer male and female; for all of you are one in Christ Jesus."

Far too many like Stephen, who have heard Jesus's words as condemnation may have missed God's joy at one of his children coming home. When I hear Jesus's response, I'm reminded of the prodigal son and the parable of the lost sheep: "No one who puts a hand to the plow and looks back is fit for the kingdom of God" (Luke 9:62). Halleluiah! Because when Elisha went home, it wasn't to return to the life he's always known, it was because he was ready to say goodbye. He didn't put his hand to the plow and look back when God called—he smashed the plow to bits and threw a party before he left. I bet Jesus smiled just thinking about Elisha, and anyone who would so extravagantly commit themselves to leaving their old home and following God to a new one.

Where Is Your Home?

Where is your home? This is the question I asked Stephen and one that I continue to ask myself.

It's estimated that "40 percent of homeless youth identify as LGBTQ+."[9] The reason Stephen found it as difficult to come out to fam-

---

9. Human Rights Campaign, "LGBTQ Youth Homelessness," hrc.org., accessed June 26, 2019, www.hrc.org/resources/lgbt-youth-homelessness.

ily, as I did, is that home isn't always a safe place, especially for LGBTQ+ folk. An unsafe home is the reason Jesus wants to create a new home for his followers—a home built on loving-kindness. God wants *hesed* to be revealed through ordinary people today just as it was in Ruth's day. But it isn't an easy task. Even God didn't get it right the first time. God called all of creation "good" in Genesis (1:31), and a few chapters later everything turned wicked, violent, and corrupt. God doesn't expect us to always get things right. God erased it all and started over and set humankind on a path that leads to Jesus—someone who could represent that good and loving God to humankind and help us to create a home that is safe for everyone. I don't know what your home is like, or how hard you've worked to keep it or change it. But I know that God is inviting you to be a part of one that is built on love.

The first step toward home for all of us is to recognize that we are loved by God. Noah saw the worst imaginable thing happen to his world, but he did not ride out the flood waters alone. God was with him and God will be with you through your own personal apocalypse. The same promise made to Noah with a rainbow is the same promise God makes to you: you are not a mistake to be erased. *You are the beloved of God.* It may sound corny but I know that Jesus is God's rainbow to me; the sign that this promise of God is real and forever. Jesus is the one I trust to guide me home because he lets each of us follow him in our own time. He'll let you go back and say goodbye to family and break whatever you need to break, like Elisha did. You can even throw a party after if you want to. You can come out to family like Joseph did, and he'll help you recognize how the hardships in your life can turn you into a person of integrity and grace. If your first home began as Ruth's did, with poverty and racism (or any other ism), you can trust that it can also end like Ruth's did, with your new home built on the loving-kindness of God through ordinary people, maybe even people who follow Jesus.

Maybe Jesus can speak to LGBTQ+ folk so well because he was non-normative. If you want your religious mind blown, read Graham Ward's "The Displaced Body of Jesus Christ." It's a little heady so you may need to read it three times and take notes, but it is a thrilling theological read. You can find the text online if you dig for a while, but it's a part of a compilation titled *Radical Orthodoxy: A New Theology* (London: Routledge, 1999), edited by John Millbank and Catherine Pickstock, pages 163–81.

Honestly, the best suggestion I have is for you to get to know Jesus by reading about him in the Gospels (the books titled Matthew, Mark, Luke, and John in the Bible). And if you're willing, read about him with a study group (commonly called "Bible study") like the ones you can find in a local Episcopal Church or another LGBTQ+ friendly Christian community. For a list of friendly churches in your area, check out www.gaychurch.org. They have a lot of helpful resources.

Why does sex matter? This is the question former (Church of England) Archbishop of Canterbury Rowan Williams responds to in his article titled, "The Body's Grace." This essay was originally delivered as the 10th Michael Harding Memorial Address to the Lesbian and Gay Christian Movement in 1989 and has been described as "the best 10 pages written about sexuality in the twentieth century." It was subsequently collected in the volume edited by Eugene Rogers, *Theology and Sexuality* (Oxford: Blackwell, 2001), which is also an excellent read.

Did you know that the Episcopal Church was blessing queer relationships before the United States made same-sex marriages legal? And before that, queer folk were already being ordained as clergy. For the theology buffs and Bible nerds who want to learn more about the process the Episcopal Church went through in order to become affirming of those who identify as LGBTQ+, read the document titled, "Same Sex Relationships in the Life of the Church." It's in the links section on www.collegeforbishops.org/resolutions-docs.

CHAPTER 7

SEX

Samantha Clare

A couple of years after I graduated from college, I met up with a dear friend on a Friday night. Over drinks I popped the question: "What is your theology of sexuality?" This is not the typical question you expect to hear in a dive bar, but it was one that had been on the forefront of my mind for some time. There were two things I knew for certain about myself, and they still hold true: I am deeply convicted by my faith in God and I am a sexual being. Integrity and authenticity are of high value to me, so it has been incredibly important to reconcile my faith with my sexuality and to be able to articulate my beliefs and how they inform the way I choose to live in the world.

My friend's response was something like: "That's a good question." A conversation began that night and lasted for a couple of years as together we explored where sexuality and religion meet, what the church has to say about it, and what it means for our lives and the lives of others in our community.

Raised in a mostly sex-positive environment, I received comprehensive sex education in public school, my parents gave me the talk, and we even openly discussed sexuality in the church I attended. I know this isn't everyone's story, but it is mine. I am grateful for the exposure that prepared me to inhabit my sexuality. Still, by the time I was in my mid-twenties, all sorts of conflicting and problematic messages about sex had been ingrained in me. It took time and intention to dismantle and rebuild a healthy theology of sexuality. Today I feel confident in articulating my own belief system and how my own convictions fit into the understandings of the wider church.

I invite you to engage in this same work. A single chapter will not give you all the information you need, but it is a place to start exploring your ideas about sexuality and God, where they came from, and how they fit together.

Starting with Good

The church has spent a great deal of time and energy talking about what sort of sex people should or should not be having. Think of the types of messages you have heard floating around. Even if they were not directly taught to you, the fact that you are aware of them means they have had some sort of impact on you. Here are a few examples of what some people claim are sexual sins that you may have heard before: immodesty, masturbation, pornography, lust, premarital sex, the use of contraception, homosexuality, and transgender identity. I could write a whole book on each of these subjects and the development of thought in the church. The point of listing them here is to say that the way the church most often approaches sexuality attempts to control behavior from a place of guilt, fear, and shame in the name of God.

I invite you to take a different approach by recognizing the inherent goodness that God has bestowed in you. When we start here, we might end up with different conclusions than we held before, or perhaps our investigations could end with the same conclusions as before. Either way, we build a framework of understanding that honors our inherent dignity. In the Acts of the Apostles, God speaks to Peter and says: "What God has made clean, you must not call profane" (Acts 10:15). You, your body, and your sexuality are clean; you must not call any part of yourself profane. You are perfectly made by God and deserve to be treated as the whole and holy being that you are.

While many church teachings about sexuality do harm to our bodies and spirits, you have the power to leave toxic and oppressive doctrine behind. You have the ability to discern when church teachings follow the way of Jesus—which means loving God, neighbor, and self—from when they have been distorted by human agendas. God invites you to reclaim your own holiness and receive God's love, grace, and mercy. Whatever your pastor or priest said you need to do to be worthy, all the things you may have internalized about purity and sin—ask all those voices in your head to be quiet for a few minutes. Take some time before you keep reading to set down some of your baggage and that which weighs you down.

Made in the Image and Likeness of God

Let's start at the very beginning. In the story of creation, God made all things and called them good. God created your body, made you a sexual being, and called you good. When God created you in God's image, you were perfectly made. You do not need to make yourself a little less or a little more of anything. You do not need to deny your sexuality in order to be good.

Speaking of God, the psalmist writes: "For it was you who formed my inward parts; you knit me together in my mother's womb. I praise you, for I am fearfully and wonderfully made. Wonderful are your works; that I know very well" (Ps. 139:13–14). You are one of God's works and you are perfectly made. God knows you intimately. You and your sexuality were designed by God and you reflect the divine. Thus, God rejoices in your fulfillment of an authentic life.

Remember that if this is true about you, then it is true about everyone. Transgender, cisgender, lesbian, gay, bisexual, pansexual, asexual, and heterosexual people are all made in the image and the likeness of God. Our diversity reflects the nature of God, which is so vast and broad that our human minds cannot comprehend its fullness. God transcends and enfolds all genders and sexual orientations.

Therefore, there is no singular way to an authentic Christian sex life. You can be celibate or you can be sexually active. You can be provocative or modest. You can be intensely or not at all interested in sex. You can be one thing today and another tomorrow. You can follow Jesus and express your sexuality in unnumbered ways. Jesus teaches us: "'You shall love the Lord your God with all your heart, and with all your soul, and with all your mind.' This is the greatest and first commandment. And the second is like it: 'You shall love your neighbor as yourself.' On these two commandments hang all the law and the prophets" (Matt. 22:37–40).

This is the Gospel message summarized. When you accept someone's sexuality, you are loving your neighbor. When you accept your own sexuality, you are loving yourself. When you do either of these things, you are loving God, because we are all made in God's image.

Wholistic Health Integrates Sexuality

God created humans as sexual beings. No matter what others might tell you, your sexual self is not meant to be denied or compartmentalized. It is not healthy for you to cut off or deny any part of yourself. The health of one area of your life affects other aspects of your well-being. When you have a healthy and authentic relationship with sex and your sexuality, there are positive effects on your mental, physical, and spiritual health, as well as your ability to have healthy relationships with other people. Sexual health and living authentically are a part of God's plan for your life. God wants you to have a life that is integrated and fulfilling.

This approach is not unique to a Christian perspective. The World Health Organization defines sexual health as:

A state of physical, emotional, mental and social well-being in relation to sexuality; not merely the absence of disease, dysfunction or infirmity. Sexual health requires a positive and respectful approach to sexuality and sexual relationships, as well as the possibility of having pleasurable and safe sexual experiences, free of coercion, discrimination and violence. For sexual health to be attained and maintained, the sexual rights of all persons must be respected, protected and fulfilled.[1]

This definition is a helpful metric to use in examining your own sexual health. It acknowledges the intersectional nature of wellness.

Throughout life you are likely to experience some of the components of sexuality, both positive and negative, detailed in the definition above. Developing the skill to think theologically about sex will help you nav-

1. "Defining Sexual Health," The World Health Organization, WHO 2019, www .who.int/reproductivehealth/topics/sexual_health/sh_definitions/en/.

igate your own sexual health. There is a lot of ground to cover; sexual health is multifaceted. Let's explore some specific issues that arise in relation to sex and see how scripture, tradition, and reason can help us approach complex choices involving sex. Consider what you read here a starting place, an invitation to your own exploration as you discern what sort of sex life you are called to have.

Discernment for Sexual Encounters

The church gives us tools for self-examination and for reflecting on whether our choices are healthy or unhealthy. When someone is baptized in the Episcopal Church, they are asked to make a series of promises. Whether or not you were baptized as an Episcopalian, the questions are helpful rubrics for living a Christian life. In these promises we are asked: "Will you seek and serve Christ in all persons, loving your neighbor as yourself? . . . Will you strive for justice and peace among all people, and respect the dignity of every human being?"[2] These two questions provide a mirror for us to hold ourselves and our actions up to as we make choices about our bodies and sex.

When entering a complex situation, consider reflecting on the baptismal promises by asking yourself: Is the choice I am about to make an expression of love for myself and for others? Does this decision respect my dignity and the dignity of all other people who will be impacted? If the answer is yes, then you know you are listening to God's call for us to love God, our neighbors, and ourselves. If the answer is no or not fully, then consider alternative options that draw you toward the way of love.

The point of making healthy choices is not to earn God's love. God will not stop loving you for losing your virginity before marriage, for getting an abortion, or for contracting a sexually transmitted disease. Remember our discussion earlier: doctrine about sexual sin is often the product of control, shame, and guilt, rather than about the love, grace, and mercy that we believe is the nature of God. God will not love you any more if you are heterosexual, modest, or pure. There is no right or

---

2. The Book of Common Prayer, 305.

godly way to perform gender. You do not need to earn God's approval and there is nothing that you can do to separate yourself from the love of God. Nothing. God's love for us is so vast and so deep we cannot comprehend it.

Center your identity as being a beloved child of God. When you ask, "Is this an expression of love?" or "Does this respect dignity?" you are reminded that God is love and that you are worthy of love, respect, and dignity because God created you and called you good. As a Christian you are called to do all things through love and that all people share an identity as a child of God. This affords everyone love, respect, and dignity. God wants us to make healthy choices because God loves us; when we make choices that honor ourselves, each other, and all of creation, the kingdom of God is realized.

Every time you engage in a sexual act ask: is this act an expression of love? Just because you have had sex before, even with the same person, does not automatically make the answer affirmative. In this moment, will this decision affirm your dignity? God gave all people agency. It is just as important for you to be able to discern your boundaries as it is for you to listen to and honor the boundaries of other people.

This sort of self-reflection applies not only to decisions about when to have sex and whom to have sex with. It can also inform how you think and talk about your body and the bodies of other people. Using these questions can help to guide decisions about gender expression. If love and dignity are the bar, then you can choose to set aside everything the church may have taught you about what is good, right, and appropriate. You can listen to God's voice speaking through you.

There is not a singular correct answer for all people in all situations. This is part of the mystery of God's deep and incomprehensible love. Creation is beautifully diverse. We are at once unique unto ourselves and made in the image of God. What is an expression of love and an affirmation of dignity for you may not be the same for all people. There is no definitive line that can be drawn in the sand. We cannot pull out a divine checklist of sins that tells us: do this; don't do this. Instead we have to think critically and ask ourselves each and every time: Does this action upset my relationship with God? If I do this, will it warp my relationship with another person? Does this choice harm my relationship to myself or the well-being of others?

Sex Will Not Separate You from the Love of God

Another commitment we are asked to make at baptism is: "Will you persevere in resisting evil, and, whenever you fall into sin, repent and return to the Lord?"[3] Notice the wording in this question—whenever you fall into sin, not *if* you fall into sin, *whenever*. This is the human condition, and the church knows it. People make mistakes and falling short is part of being human. You are perfectly made but not perfect.

A sin is not tied to a specific behavior like having sex or being anything other than cis and straight. Sin has to do with your relationship to a thing rather than the thing itself. There are healthy ways to care for our bodies and there are unhealthy ways to misuse and abuse our bodies. Sex is not inherently sinful; it can isolate and degrade, or it can reflect the sort of loving relationship God calls us to. We sin when we choose to act in a way that distorts our relationship with God, other people, and ourselves.

Whenever we sin, whenever we are lost, we are invited to return to God. There are several parables that Jesus told to illustrate this. A shepherd with one hundred sheep loses one sheep. The shepherd leaves his flock to find the one who has gone astray. When the sheep is found the shepherd rejoices. A woman has ten coins and loses one. She searches high and low until she finds the missing one and when she finds it she celebrates. A man has two sons, the younger one demands his inheritance so that he can go off on his own, perhaps driven by his lustful sexual desires. He squanders what he has, makes choices that are sinful, and finds himself separated not only from his relationships with his family and God but even from his own dignity. He decides to return in the hopes that even a fraction of his life will be restored. He is welcomed home by his father with an abundance of love.

Now seems like as appropriate a time as any to drop in the following side note. One part of developing a theological framework for sexuality,

---

3. Ibid., 304.

or anything, is digging into scripture. Pull out your Bible and read these stories for yourself. This is an important thing to do anytime someone uses scripture to teach you something. Sure, I am telling you one way to read these stories. But there are others too. When you engage the material firsthand, you will have different takeaways that help inform your understanding in a well-rounded way. The stories we are discussing here can be found in the Gospel of Luke.[4]

Jesus uses these three parables to teach the reader that God seeks you and waits for you to return. God will keep on loving you, no matter what choices you've made and no matter what choices you make going forward. Making a choice you are not proud of does not make you a bad person. You are more than the decisions that you make. There is no sin great enough to separate us from the infinite and incomprehensible love of God. Repentance is not about earning God's love; it is about acknowledging there was a breach in the covenant you've made with God and seeking to restore the relationship. When you sin, you have the opportunity to confess, seek forgiveness, and recommit yourself to your covenant with God. Grace and forgiveness are born out of God's unconditional love for us.

Dwell in the knowledge that God has a loving relationship with humanity. Loving relationships are not controlling or manipulative. As our human relationships are meant to model our relationship with God, we are called to mutual concern for each other's whole selves. Our relationships ought to be informed by loving kindness, respect, and dignity.

Just as God does not force anyone to love God, you should not force anyone to love you. When you take advantage of another person, physically or otherwise, you disrespect their God-given dignity. God gave humans the ability to choose, and so consent is important to God. God has given each of us agency, and we are called to respect that in ourselves and in others. This means claiming and using our own voices and listening to and honoring the voice of others. Consent cannot be implied, and it requires communication throughout the entire activity. Consent is about more than permission or submission: it should be affirmative and

---

4. These parables can be found in Luke 15:3–7; 15:8–10; and 15:11–32 respectively.

enthusiastic. Sexual activity involving two people should involve mutual interest, investment, and care.

Resisting Unhealthy Relationships with Sex

Sex is not designed to be transactional. Human beings are not commodities to be traded. When you start to approach sex or your body as something you can give in expectation of receiving something in return, you undermine the inherent value and worth God has instilled in each person. Your body is a holy temple. God dwells in you. God dwells in all people. Bodies are sometimes turned into commodities through pornography and sex work. These things are not inherently evil by definition, but they can and often do degrade people.

The idea that God created humans as subjects, not objects, is countercultural. From a young age we are taught to objectify bodies and to ascribe value to specific, often unattainable, ideals. We are told the lie that beauty and worth are tied to a certain weight, height, or skin tone. Forces outside of our control infiltrate our consciousness and persuade us to think that there are lines that separate good bodies from bad bodies and that desirability is limited to a certain type of body. Remember, God made all bodies good and created a diversity of bodies that are all of equal value and worth.

Devastatingly, we live in a world where these truths are affronted. Some people find themselves in situations where their agency is stripped from them, without the ability to use their own voices or make their own decisions. The gift God gives humans with the freedom of choice is a great blessing, but it is also the reason evil exists. People make choices that are not rooted in love and cause suffering in the lives of others. If we believe that God is good, we must also affirm that evil is not of God. God does not cause pain or punish people. We may not be able to find an answer to why people suffer, but we can rest assured that God's loving presence is always with us.

Rape, incest, sex trafficking, molestation, assault, harassment, and abuse are never a part of God's plan. If you are the victim of sexual violence, there is nothing you did to cause your suffering. No one can take away your God-given goodness. God always loves you and will keep on loving you no matter what. Your abuser cannot take that away from you. These few words might offer some solace, even if only for a moment, but they are not enough. You deserve healing and wholeness. If you have sexual trauma, you have the right to seek professional help and spiritual care.[5] You are not alone.

Sexual Health and Well-Being

All human life is sacred, including yours, from inception until death. As such, abortion ought not be used as a means of birth control and is not a decision to be entered into lightly. Still, we live in a world corrupted by injustice and sexual violence.[6] Some pregnancies are the result of rape, while others are life-threatening. Not all people have access to sex education or contraception. Legislating and condemning abortion or sex workers does not address these root issues. As Christians, we are called to work to repair the breach in our society so that all people can have access to contraceptives and sexuality education and to end all forms of sexual abuse so that the need for abortion procedures ceases to exist. In the meantime, God loves everyone, and this includes people who get abortions.

All people have the right to access reproductive health care as a means of caring for their physical and sexual health. This is an integral part of affirming the dignity and worth of all human beings. This means access to contraception, preventative care, mental health services, and much more. In order to be good stewards of creation, we need access to the resources that make care possible.

As you steward your own sexual health, keep in mind that sexuality and sexual expression can change throughout a person's life. God gave us the gift of choice and the blessing of continual growth. You can expect

---

5. Many communities have local sexual trauma recovery services. If you don't know where to start looking, consider national organizations such as www.rainn.org.

6. If you want to know more about the Episcopal Church's stance on abortion and reproductive health, here is a helpful guide: www.episcopalchurch.org/posts/ogr/summary-general-convention-resolutions-abortion-and-womens-reproductive-health.

things to change. Your body will change. Your desires, your interest in sexual activity, and what you are attracted to will change.

You don't have to figure it all out right now, but you are invited to take an active role in your own sexual and spiritual formation. In the account of creation in Genesis, God entrusts humankind as stewards of creation and to take dominion over the earth and all life upon it. On the sixth day "God blessed them, and God said to them, 'Be fruitful and multiply, and fill the earth and subdue it; and have dominion . . . over every living thing that moves upon the earth.' . . . And it was so. God saw everything that he had made, and indeed, it was very good" (Gen. 1:28, 30–31). We are made responsible for the care of all living things, which includes ourselves and our own bodies. In order to be good stewards of creation, we are required to pay attention to, nurture, and cultivate our sexual health.

Distorted ideas about sex and sexuality fester both inside and outside the Church, but as people of faith we have a responsibility to counter the forces of evil in the world that tell us we are not enough. As Christians, we profess faith in unconditional love and inherent goodness. We are called to proclaim good news and transform unjust structures. The Episcopal Church has stated its responsibility to provide a safe, hospitable environment for frank conversation about human sexuality, to share and teach accurate information, and to promote dialogue.[7] You have a right to demand this be made a reality in your local faith community. It is imperative to your spiritual well-being that you seek out sexual education. Because God created humans to be in relationship with one another, it is also good to do this in community. Find a friend who can be a dialogue partner with you for open and nonjudgmental conversation while you both learn. Visit your campus health center or local resource centers if available. Seek out a spiritual guide, priest, or campus minister but remember that they too are human and do not have all the answers, especially the specific answers for yourself that you will seek. If none of these options are available, you might try finding community online.

---

7. General Convention, *Journal of the General Convention of . . . The Episcopal Church, Denver, 2000* (New York: General Convention, 2001), 202, https://episcopal archives.org/cgi-bin/acts/acts_resolution.pl?resolution=2000-A046.

As you dig into this work, you are probably going to have very specific questions about passages from the Bible, the teachings of our ancestors in the faith, or things you heard in youth group or Sunday school. There are lots of helpful resources out to help dismantle the toxic, sexist, patriarchal, shaming, and guilt-ridden ideas about sex and sexuality that get engrained in us by the church and society. There are also many harmful resources. Be critical of the sources you engage. Ask yourself whether what you are learning affirms what you know about God's good and loving nature. Remember God gave you the gift of reason.

Going Deeper A few good places to start might be:

- Leslie Choplin and Jenny Beaumont's *These Are Our Bodies: Talking Faith & Sexuality at Church & Home* (Church Publishing, 2016) gives a theological, ethical, and developmental overview of human sexuality.

- Nadia Bolz-Weber's *Shameless: A Sexual Revolution* (Convergent, 2019) dismantles ideas about sex, shame, guilt, and the church.

- Rob Bell's *Sex God: Exploring the Endless Connections between Sexuality and Spirituality* (HarperCollins, 2012) is a helpful overview but should be read critically in regards to gender and sexual orientation.

- The Planned Parenthood website has comprehensive evidence-based sex education resources. www.plannedparenthood.org/.

- According to Title IX, it is illegal to discriminate based on sex in education programs or activities that receive federal financial assistance. More information can be found here: www2.ed.gov /about/offices/list/ocr/docs/tix_dis.html.

CHAPTER 8

PARTYING

Ben Adams

We have become accustomed to late nights at the University of Chicago hospital emergency room (ER). Tara and I have been there many times before with students for various ailments, but the most common ER visits are alcohol related. As "resident heads" at the University of Chicago, we knew that accompanying students to the ER, for whatever reason, is what we signed up for, but it never made the 2:00 a.m. alcohol transport phone call any easier to get out of bed for. On a particularly cold winter night, we received one such call.

Our resident had already arrived at the hospital via the ambulance; when I walked in they were in the waiting room passed out, but sitting up in a wheelchair. This resident had been found on the Midway, a greenspace on the south edge of campus, on the ground, passed out, and it was evident as they had dirt all over their face as well as the nice clothes they had on from earlier that night. After a half hour or so we were called back to the room for evaluation, just as this resident finally started to come to. When asked for identification, this resident patted their pockets only to realize that their wallet was gone. It turned out that they were also robbed as they were passed out. As more of the story came out, it was revealed that this resident had been pressured at the fancy Greek life party they attended to "go vertical," which means that they had to keep a bottle of liquor vertical as they drank for as long as their friends around them were singing a particular song. After some time of this, the resident faintly recalled a physical altercation between them and another partygoer. The hosts of the party then asked this resident to leave. The resident obliged with the host's request and attempted to make it home on their own, but passed out during the walk, fell facedown, and were lucky to be found quickly given the cold Chicago winter temperatures.

Several hours later in the ER, after the resident had been given an IV with some fluids and regained full consciousness, we were given the green light to leave the hospital. I escorted the resident back to the dorm. The next day we set up a time to chat. The conversation could have easily been a "WHAT WERE YOU THINKING!?" kind of conversation, but we took a different approach. We talked about what led up to the events of that night, what decisions were made, and how can we plan for a better party experience in the future. It was both a chance to reflect on how things went so poorly and how practicing more intention next time could result in a more positive experience.

Ultimately this resident endured no long-term injuries from their fraught night of partying and they were able to replace most of the things that were stolen from them. Maybe the hardest part of it all for them was explaining the costly ambulance ride to their parents. Most of all, this moment served as a turning point for this resident. From that moment onward, this resident's relationship to partying and alcohol became more balanced.

I don't tell you this story to scare you. I'm not trying to convince you not to party, because most experiences of partying do not end up like this. Rather, I hope this story can serve as our starting point from which we can begin to thoughtfully engage the reality of partying in college with a sense of faithfulness and balance. I hope to equip you with some practical and theological tools to help you make decisions about partying from a place of belovedness. Being both a campus pastor and living on a college campus in a dorm has prepared me with a unique perspective that can help shed some light on our conversation about partying; I've accompanied many students as they navigate the college party scene. But even more important than both of those roles is that I too was once a college freshman (way back in 2005) making choices about partying. I can't say that I always got it right, but I do have wisdom from my own experience that I hope will be useful.

In the opening story, the resident lost track of their belovedness in the midst of peer pressure, and as a result, made poor decisions. To me, belovedness means that there's nothing you can do to make God love you more and there's nothing you can do to make God love you less. You are loved just as you are. No. Matter. What. I heard this once from a beloved colleague of mine, Tom Gaulke, and he told me that he heard it from his beloved pastor growing up. So I am a third-generation pastor using this definition of belovedness; even though it's not an original definition, it was quite remarkable the first time I heard belovedness defined this way. Previously I knew that God loved me, but I always had this sneaking feeling that I could lose that love with bad behavior, or earn more of it with good behavior. Who knew that the truth of God's love was way simpler and more graceful than that? I need that good news of unmerited and unending love in my life, and I suspect that you do too. A divine love that you can't do anything to gain or lose.

The Facts

Surveying the landscape of the campus wilderness, we often fixate on what is portrayed to be the central part of the college experience—the parties. This idea has been pervasive, especially in American culture for many years, and has been encouraged by American media ever since the 1978 release of the movie *Animal House.* Since then, students have been trying to imitate the party habits they've seen on screen.

But is *Animal House* a realistic standard or an accurate picture of what college life and parties actually look like? Are parties like the ones on the silver screen an inevitable or even common part of college life? The simple answer to those questions is *no.* College is not an endless drunken social. In fact, for most, partying in college makes up a smaller percentage of the experience than in years past. Wild stereotypes about college abound, but if we turn our attention to the data, it doesn't support these false narratives.

A nationwide report released in 2015 found that today's students are spending less time partying. These findings came from a study on national norms of the American college freshman that surveyed more than 150,000 freshmen at 227 four-year colleges in the United States. The researchers from the University of California, Los Angeles, found that over the past twenty-seven years, self-reported rates of time spent socializing in person with others have essentially flipped: in 1987, 37.9 percent of incoming freshmen socialized at least 16 hours per week with friends, while 18.1 percent socialized for 5 hours or less. By 2014, those figures were 18 percent for freshmen who socialized at least 16 hours per week with friends and 38.8 percent for students who socialized for 5 hours or less—an all-time low and an all-time high, respectively.[1]

There are many factors that contribute to this shift. Social media and technology connects us more in a virtual and not a physical way. The growing amount of student loan debt being taken on by students precludes them from partying as much due to their heightened concern of getting a high-paying job after graduation to pay off their student loans. Whatever the factors, the truth remains that the *Animal House* portrayal of college is misleading.

This isn't to say that partying doesn't happen. It does. According to the 2016 National Survey on Drug Use and Health, 57.2 percent of full-time college students ages 18 to 22 drank alcohol in the past month; 38 percent engaged in binge drinking (5 or more drinks on a single occasion for men or 4 or more drinks on an occasion for women) in the past month; and 10.5 percent engaged in heavy alcohol use (binge drinking on five or more days in the past month). These rates are higher than those of their non-college-attending peers.[2]

For many attending college, this is their first time being exposed to drugs and alcohol at parties, leading to definite risks involved if one decides to partake. There are academic consequences: one in four students say their academic performance has suffered from drinking. Beyond that,

1. Andrew Giambrone, "Are College Students Partying Less?" *The Atlantic*, February 10, 2015, www.theatlantic.com/education/archive/2015/02/are-college-students -partying-less/385326/.

2. Substance Abuse and Mental Health Services Administration, *Key Substance Use and Mental Health Indicators in the United States: Results from the 2016 National Survey on Drug Use and Health (HHS Publication No. SMA 17-5044, NSDUH Series H-52)* (Rockville, MD: Center for Behavioral Health Statistics and Quality, Substance Abuse and Mental Health Services Administration, 2017), www.samhsa.gov/data /sites/default/files/NSDUH-FFR1-2016/NSDUH-FFR1-2016.htm.

the most recent statistics from the National Institute on Alcohol Abuse and Alcoholism indicate that drinking by college students ages 18 to 24 is involved in an estimated 1,519 student deaths each year, an estimated 696,000 assaults by another student who has been drinking, and 97,000 cases of sexual assault or date rape each year.[3] These statistics might seem to contradict what we said earlier about college partying being on the decline, but even though partying and socializing is decreasing, signs are that partying is getting even harder. More students are caught up in a work hard / play hard bingeing culture where their one intention for drinking is to get drunk. They do this by choosing hard liquor over beer, and they are drinking, or predrinking/pregaming in advance of social events. Many even report their goal of drinking is to black out.[4]

Now these numbers and statistics can never tell the full story, but they can help to demystify the college experience and paint for you an accurate picture of the college partying landscape. Additionally, I'd like to say, choosing to party in college doesn't make you bad, and choosing not to doesn't make your college experience deficient or invalid. Remember beloveds, there is nothing you can do to make God love you more, and there is nothing you can do to make God love you less, you are loved just as you are.

What Does the Bible Say?

Let us now dive into scripture for wisdom on partying. Spoiler alert: the Bible does not give us a clear answer either way about whether or not we should party. Like a seesaw, once you think you've got one side pinned down, the other side pops up. For example, in Galatians 5:19–21 or 1 Corinthians 6:9–10, drunkards and drunkenness are listed along with other

3. "Fall Semester—A Time for Parents to Discuss the Risks of College Drinking," National Institute on Alcohol Abuse and Alcoholism, June 26, 2019. www.niaaa.nih .gov/publications/brochures-and-fact-sheets/time-for-parents-discuss-risks-college -drinking.

4. Beth Mcmurtrie, "Why Colleges Haven't Stopped Binge Drinking," *The New York Times*, December 14, 2014, www.nytimes.com/2014/12/15/us/why-colleges -havent-stopped-binge-drinking.html.

wrongdoers and wrongdoings that will cause us to not inherit the king-dom of God. While on one side of the scriptural seesaw, we read these warnings against drunkenness, the other side of the scriptural seesaw gives us phrases like "Eat, drink, and be merry!" or psalms like Psalm 104, where God is celebrated for bringing forth wine to gladden our hearts. Even Jesus knows that no party can go without wine, so at the wedding at Cana he turns water into wine so the guests can continue to turn up (John 2:1–11). We could even consider the Last Supper that Jesus shares with his disciples before his crucifixion as a dinner party amongst good friends complete with good wine and bread. Maybe that's a way we could con-tinue to think of the communion we share in worship together: the dinner party that Jesus instituted that never ends, complete with good food and drinks, where there's nothing we can bring to the party except ourselves, everyone gets enough, and we are left satisfied yet hungry for justice.

That is nowhere near an exhaustive list of references to partying in the Bible, but even with just a small snapshot, it's evident that the back and forth seesaw action of scripture never gives us a definitive answer on whether or not we should party. The bottom line is that there are both positive things that are said about alcohol consumption at parties and there are warnings about excessive consumption. Then what wisdom does scripture have for us when we're in that place and we have to decide what end of the seesaw we'd like to sit at?

For that let's open our Bibles to 1 Corinthians. This is a book of the Bible that was actually a letter to the Church in Corinth (think south-cen-tral Greece), written by Paul. Paul wrote this letter to the church in Corinth because they were struggling mightily. Douglas Campbell states it plainly when he says, "The church at Corinth was a mess." Campbell goes on to say, "When we take a step back from all the ins and outs of the issues in the letter, we can see that Paul is urging something simple on the Corinthians. A great deal of what he says can be summed up in the phrase 'appropriate relating.'"[5]

5. Douglas A. Campbell "Paul Wrote 1 Corinthians to a Community in the Middle of a Culture War," *The Christian Century,* December 22, 2019, www.christiancentury.org /article/critical-essay/paul-wrote-1-corinthians-community-middle-culture-war.

I love that phrase "appropriate relating." It could apply to our human relationships and how we treat one another, it can apply to our relationship to our own bodies and how we regard them, it could apply to our relationship to God, or it could apply to our relationship to the things around us and how we use them for life-giving purposes or not. But "appropriate relating" is not always black and white, and things get messy easily when it comes to human relationships, body image, God, and stuff, so how do we navigate the gray area? First Corinthians 6:12 offers to us this beautiful wisdom: "'All things are lawful for me,' but not all things are beneficial. 'All things are lawful for me, but I will not be dominated by anything.'"

What if we took that verse and applied it to our conversation about partying? This passage tells us that legality, or our ability to get away with something without negative repercussions, can no longer be our standard. Paul is challenging us to consider how beneficial the things around us are and how dominant they potentially are over us. Therefore, "appropriately relating" to partying means setting a new standard beyond legality, and stopping to ask ourselves two questions:

1. Is this beneficial to me?

2. Am I in control?

These questions help us clarify whether partying is beneficial and whether or not we are being dominated by partying itself. With both of these standards for appropriate relating, there is a line. Everyone's line is a little different. If we cross it, we are no longer partying in a way that benefits ourselves and others. If we cross it, we lose control, and drugs and alcohol take control of us and dominate us. Even though partying in college might be lawful (for those of you who are of age), or at least culturally acceptable for the rest of you, there is a line that we must walk in order for our desires to remain beneficial and controlled. Walking that line with precision requires intention. Someone balancing on a tightrope can't walk across without placing each foot in front of the other with great intention. Similarly, when we party, we should take each step with intention and find our balance. When we are balanced, we are in control, and when we internally reflect before making decisions, we are not being dominated by external people or substances.

More than any of these specific verses of scripture that we can reference, it's the overall message of the Bible that reminds us of our belovedness. After all, the Bible is a love story. When we reflect on the love that God has for us by becoming one with us in Jesus Christ, dying to liberate us and rising to save us, scripture makes it abundantly clear that we are loved beyond all measure. From the place of belovedness, our lives are a response to God's eternal love for us. The good news revealed in Jesus Christ is that there is nothing we can do to make God love us more and there is nothing we can do to make God love us less. We are all beloved just the way we are. Decisions about partying made out of a place of trust in this good news that the Bible tells will yield loving, life-giving results. You are a part of God's love story, let that guide your way.

Getting Back on the Seesaw

Earlier I mentioned the scriptural seesaw, the back and forth wisdom that scripture offers us. I'd like to run with that image even further, but this time apply it to our social lives. Imagine with me for a minute the playground you grew up playing on as a kid. Remember riding a seesaw on that playground? Remember how each side would go up and down as each person pushed off the ground, pulling the other person back down? Hold that image of riding a seesaw in your mind as we reflect on what partying in college could look like. Start with what a less than beloved approach to partying could look like—we'll call that bingeing. To binge is to indulge in an activity to excess. Binge culture is prominent in society and magnified on college campuses. The work hard / play hard mentality is embraced by many in college, and students can really hurt themselves and others as a result. On the college social life seesaw, this approach to partying might start out exciting for each rider on the seesaw, but over time as the bingeing experience intensifies, so does the speed at which both the people on the seesaw are moving, each rider crashing to the ground harder and being sent up faster, until one or both of the riders either fall off, hurt themselves, or throw up. Newton's Third

Law, "For every action, there is an equal and opposite reaction," is on full display as the seesaw moves up and down. But just because the seesaw moves with equal reaction, is a wildly moving seesaw a good example of balance?

I'd argue it isn't. Because maintaining balance through extreme action to counteract the original action creates overcorrections and throws off our balance altogether. That's bingeing. Excessive studying requiring a night of excessive partying to take the edge off is not going to leave us feeling healthy or balanced. Instead we end up more exhausted and drained than when we first began.

So let's instead imagine a more balanced seesaw. Picture one in your mind that is perfectly flat and level with the ground. Then add some riders. As the first one gets on, their side goes down, but then as the second rider gets on, the seesaw returns to parallel with the ground. The careful mount of the first rider is gently matched by the second. Then if one decides to move the seesaw, they do so with attention paid to their partner rider. Care and concern for each rider's fun and well-being is considered and if one rider requests to stop riding, their request is received and honored by the other rider.

Maybe the balanced version of the seesaw that's moving more gently is less exciting, but each rider is much less likely to fall off, get hurt, or throw up. The same is true when we look at party culture. If we take the approach of making our choices from a place of belovedness, then we must acknowledge that balance is beloved and bingeing is not. When we equate our enjoyment of a party with excitement, we risk losing our sense of belovedness and others for a thrill, but if we can maintain a commitment to making sure that our own and other's enjoyment of a party doesn't have to come at each other's expense, then we can make both fun and faithful choices.

What I love most about the seesaw metaphor for bingeing or balance is that it involves two people. Partying is a social experience and an important one in the college experience as we seek to form friendships, find romantic partners, and participate in community. In the beloved community we understand that our experience is interrelated, our decisions impact others in both positive and negative ways, and much like riding a seesaw, we must be attentive to one another and intentional about our choices to maintain that beloved community.[6]

When I think about a party in my own experience where I failed to exercise this ethic of balanced belovedness, it would be my bachelor party. With just a week to go before I was to marry the love of my life, I walked into my bachelor party, gave in to the peer pressure from my friends and family at the party, and proceeded to drink eight shots of Jim Beam within the first half hour. Needless to say, I lost consciousness shortly after, slammed my head on a table leg, threw up everywhere, and passed out until 2:30 p.m. the next day. I had not gracefully got on or dismounted from the seesaw. Instead, I jumped on with two feet and was immediately thrown off.

My decision to take the eight shots of whiskey was not made from a place of belovedness. I did not consider my own beloved body and well-being, and I did not consider the impact of my choices on the other beloved guests of the party, the other riders on the seesaw. I decided to take the shots because of the peer pressure I felt; I let my ego respond to the challenge that I was being faced with. It is fair to say that the encouragement and pressure from the other guests at the party was also not abiding by an ethic of belovedness. They weren't looking out for my best interest but had instead tried to live up to some flawed idea that the point of a bachelor party was to get the bachelor as messed up as possible.

As a result of both the pressure I felt and my choice to give into that pressure, my experience of my bachelor party was neither fun nor faithful. I ended up being a huge liability to the other guests at my party, and I didn't even get to enjoy the party myself because I binged and blacked out so soon. I didn't follow an ethic of belovedness at my bachelor party, but what about a time in my life when it was?

Let's fast forward just a week later at my actual wedding. At *this* party, I made fun, faithful, beloved choices. I was able to drink, but with ade-

---

6. If you or someone you know is "partying" by themselves, please see the resource section at the end of chapter, or talk to someone you trust for help.

quate meals and water in between to keep me balanced all night. I had a great time dancing, socializing, and enjoying my first married moments with Tara. I did rip my pants on the dance floor, but that's more evidence to support the fact that faithful partying can be fun. In fact, it was the best night of my life because I was present the whole time in body, mind, and spirit. I maintained beloved balance, I danced with my beloved, and we were surrounded by our beloved friends and family. That night, no one fell off the seesaw. We had a great time while being attentive to one another and intentional about our decisions. It was balanced, beautiful, and in a word: beloved.

Embodied Belovedness

But let's take this even a step further. Beyond the practical reasons and stories that prove *why* balanced partying is better for us and the people we are partying with, there are *theological* reasons as well. Take Jesus: he is God who took on flesh and dwelt among us. Jesus had a real body just like ours; Jesus shared in our fragile, beloved, createdness. Our bodies are redeemed and sacred.

Your body, my body, we are all members of Christ's earthly, physical, beloved body. Each time we participate in the feast of communion, we receive Christ's body and we are reminded that we leave that communion table a part of that broken, beloved, body of Christ for the sake of the world. Our createdness is sacramental and we should regard our own bodies with the same sacramental reverence that we would the body and blood of Christ in communion.

Abiding by this theology with regards to partying means that our bodies are filled with God's incarnate presence. In this light, our decisions to consume drugs and alcohol at parties should be done with care, intention, and reverence for our good and holy bodies. Choosing not to consume drugs and alcohol in light of this theology is a blessed and faithful decision as well.

Making sound, safe, and sacred choices by exercising our bodily autonomy is how our belovedness is embodied. Discipleship then can look like encouraging others to make similar life-giving choices when partying. It's important to surround yourself with people you can trust and vice-versa. After all, good friends make for beloved parties.

My hope and prayer for your college experience is that you find a beloved, balanced relationship to partying and that our reflection together in this chapter has equipped you with some scriptural, practical, and theological resources to guide you in your college experience. This starts with you, but it can be helped or hurt by the community you surround yourself with. Don't be afraid to remove yourself from less than life-giving situations and relationships. You are beloved, your body is holy and sacred, and you have autonomy over it. Most of all, your choice to party or not to party will not make God love you more or less, but rooted in this truth, good fruit will grow in your life.

Going Deeper College life can be messy and our beloved balance is easily thrown off. In these moments we can find ourselves or our friends in real trouble if bingeing becomes our default party setting. What then can you do if you or a friend finds herself in this place? What resources are available to us to help when the party culture has consumed us or the power of drugs and alcohol have started to dominate us?

Some places to start could be your campus student health center, the on-campus counselling center, a campus nurse (on call or in person), your campus pastor, a resident assistant, a trusted professor, or academic advisor; in more serious cases, the dean of students should be notified. If the situation is emergent and people seem to be in danger as a result of their partying decisions, police or EMS should be called and an ambulance should be sent to evaluate and potentially transport yourself or a friend to the hospital for help.

But let's say you just want to research some things about college life and partying on your own. For that I suggest *The Her Campus Guide to College Life* (Simon and Schuster, 2019) by Stephanie

Kaplan Lewis, Annie Chandler Wang, Windsor Hanger Western, and the Writers & Editors of *Her Campus*. Online, I found Value Colleges page on partying to be helpful: www.valuecolleges.com/guides/party -smart-navigating-the-college-party-scene/.

Finally, if substance abuse is becoming an issue that is taking over, long-term or intensive drug or alcohol treatment services should be utilized. To refer yourself or a friend, you can call the Substance Abuse and Mental Health Services Administration (SAMHSA) national helpline at 1-800-662-HELP (4357). This number is free, confidential, 24/7, 365-day-a-year treatment referral and information service (in English and Spanish) for individuals and families facing mental and/or substance use disorders. You can access their online resources as well at www.samhsa.gov/.

Don't hesitate to use these resources even if you're unsure about whether or not you need them. Ultimately, whether or not you choose to party, my prayer for you is that you make that choice deeply grounded in the truth that you are God's beloved, and there's nothing you can do to make God love you more, and there's nothing you can do to make God love you less, for you are fully and completely loved just the way you are.

CHAPTER 9

MENTAL HEALTH

David Finnegan-Hosey

I learned from college students how to speak truthfully about mental health struggles.[1]

It was the spring semester of 2012, and I had returned from a brief jaunt through hell. The previous summer I had, with the help of friends, admitted myself into the hospital for the first time in my life . . . and then the second and third time as well. By that third short-term hospitalization, it was clear that the mental health crisis I was in the midst of required an even more structured environment for healing and recovery. I found myself in a 3-month residential program, further from home, where I received a new diagnosis that seemed to make some sense of the pain I was in, a new regimen of medication, and new forms of therapy that taught me new skills for managing the nearly deadly emotional storm that had raged internally for, at that point, six whole months.

When I came back home to Washington, DC, I was safer, more stable, and grateful to be alive. All of that was true, and good. But also, things were really, really hard for a really long time.

Prior to checking myself in to the hospital, I had completed my first year of seminary and was scheduled to begin my internship in ministry with college students at the university just next door. I'd interviewed, met student leaders, and even been able to attend their opening worship service before I landed back in the hospital. Then I left town for the residential hospital program. Now that I was back home in DC, I learned

---

1. Parts of this chapter are also included in chapter 7 of David Finnegan-Hosey's *Grace Is a Pre-existing Condition: Faith, Systems, and Mental Health* (Church Publishing, 2020).

that my seminary wanted me to stay on medical leave; I was unsure when I would be able to resume classes. My days seemed unstructured. Getting out of bed was hard anyway, especially in the gloom of my basement apartment, and it often wasn't obvious what I might be getting out of bed *for*. So it came as a blessing to me that the campus ministry and its sponsoring congregation extended me an invitation to begin working with them again in the interim. I wasn't sure what I would have to offer (me, who was struggling just to get upright in the morning), but it was a reason to get out of the dark apartment, and I leapt at the chance.

Well, ok. Leapt is a bit much. I sort of crawled at the chance.

As I said, I'd already met some of the students I would be in ministry with, and so I stepped into my new role as "The Intern" a little bit unsure who knew where I'd been and what had been going on with me. It did feel as if I owed some sort of explanation as to why I had shown up in August and then disappeared by September only to reappear in January, and lying about it seemed like it would be, frankly, exhausting. So at the first Thursday night worship service that I was scheduled to lead, I gave a sermon where I talked a bit about my experiences. I talked about Jesus calling the disciples his friends, loneliness, and God understanding our lonely experiences. And I hoped that the students would know that I was ok, that they didn't have to worry about me, and that we could get back to the work of ministry that we were supposed to be doing together.

But that wasn't what happened. What happened, instead, is that students started coming to me, one at a time, and saying things like:

"I struggle with anxiety and depression, and . . ."

or

"I've got a family member with a serious mental illness, and . . . "

or

"I've got a friend who is going through a really hard time right now, and I'm not sure what to call it or how to help them, and . . ."

"and . . ." "and . . ." "and . . ." " . . . and I didn't know we could talk about it in church. But now you have, so now I know we can."

And that's how college students began the long, steady process of teaching me how to tell the truth about mental health, mental illness, and faith.

Stumbling into Story

Looking back at that time, it seems to me that I stumbled into story—stumbled into discovering the power of story, and the power of creating space for others to share their own stories, stories that they had, previously, not been sure whether they were allowed to share. If I had the chance, there are things I probably would have done differently. It was a risky move, telling that story so soon. I've learned much since then about what is healthy for me to share and not share, about the care I take with language, about being sure I've spent some time processing difficult experiences before bringing them into a sermon with me. But in all its imperfection and messiness, those first stuttering attempts to share some of my story of mental health challenges with my students opened the doorway for conversations, real conversations, about the hard stuff that we all deal with. Hard stuff that, we are increasingly aware, you, as college students, deal with regularly.

The data on mental health struggles in the college years is there for the viewing. A recent report from the American College Health Association reveals that in 2018, more than 80 percent of college students had felt overwhelmed by all they had to do, and more than 50 percent experienced feelings of hopelessness; perhaps more telling, more than 40 percent of college students reported feeling so depressed that functioning was difficult, and more than 10 percent of students shared that they had seriously considered suicide during the past year.[2] There are plenty of explanations advanced, both popularly and in academic research, for this challenging landscape, from theories of societal anxiety—growing up in a post-9/11 world deeply impacted by the financial crash of 2008; to the acknowledgment that efforts to challenge stigma around mental illness will inevitably mean higher rates of reporting, a positive hidden

---

2. American College Health Association, American College Health Association-National College Health Assessment II: Reference Group Executive Summary Fall 2018 (Silver Spring, MD: ACHA, 2018), www.acha.org/documents/ncha /NCHA-II_Fall_2018_Reference_Group_Executive_Summary.pdf.

within a seeming negative; to increased expectations on students linked to increasing college costs. Of course, college has always been a time of transition, and it's one in which the support networks and life rhythms you're used to from high school disappear and change. This can be particularly challenging because the high school and college years are when certain types of mood disorders tend to manifest themselves, so the shift in support systems comes at the same time as the emergence of a new mental health challenge. And let's face it: school can just be stressful. For some students used to excelling in school, college can be more academically challenging than they're used to; for others, the academic environment fails to live up to the high expectations they've placed on it.

Of course, college can also be an exciting and deeply meaningful time. As others in this book emphasize, college is a time for exploring who you are, what you are passionate about, and how you understand the world. It's a time for learning that the *you* you are becoming is loved by God, and discovering the type of communities and activities that help form you into the person God created you to be. But these exciting and meaningful aspects of college can bring up their own challenges to mental and emotional health. Exploring our identities can be scary, especially if we discover parts of ourselves that we have previously buried, silenced, or kept hidden from parents or other authority figures. Exploring our beliefs, our sexuality, our ability to make decisions, and then figuring out where that fits in with where (and who) we've come from is tough stuff to navigate. It's tough for me at age thirty-five; it was tough for me at eighteen; it's ok if it's tough for you. And too, sometimes the gap between the experience college is "supposed to be" and the experience you're actually having can be difficult. I've spoken to many students who have told me that they feel like they "should" be having a great time, making tons of new friends, learning so much about themselves and the world, and instead they feel a strange mix of under- and overwhelmed, which in turn comes with feelings of guilt or shame: why am I not having the amazing experience other people are having and that I'm supposed to be having?

That's why it's so important for us to have places to share honestly about the experiences we are having: the good and the bad, the struggles and the celebrations. It's important to have space for stories, not just for numbers and theories. After all, I am guessing that if you are reading this, you actually don't need the numbers to know that college can be as tough as it can be exciting. I'm guessing too that if you are reading this you are less interested in one or another explanation for why the college years are hard on students' mental health, and you are more interested in how to make it through, or to help your friend(s) make it through, a reality that is far from theoretical and that is, in fact, sitting leadenly on your dorm room floor.

If that's the case, let's take a risk, and stumble into story together—into honest storytelling about the mental health challenges that college can present, yes; but also into new stories, healing stories, that can perhaps offer some hope or at least some touch points to steady us through the stumbling.

Sharing Stories with Jesus

The apostles gathered around Jesus, and told him all that they had done and taught. (Mark 6:30)

I've forgotten, at this point, who first pointed out to me that this short verse in Mark's gospel says that the apostles told Jesus *all* they had done and taught. Read this verse aloud with different tones, and it seems to mean different things: maybe the disciples got together with Jesus and tried to outdo each other with tales of heroic acts of faith, demon-exorcising successes, and miraculous healing, which would seem to fit with an earlier verse: "They cast out many demons, and anointed with oil many who were sick and cured them" (Mark 6:13). But maybe they were more honest. Maybe they talked about their failures and shortcomings. This would seem to fit as well, with this verse following as it does the story of Jesus totally bombing in his own hometown, calling the disciples at a time when Jesus's mission wasn't off to a great start, immediately followed by the gruesome execution of John the Baptist, a friend and ally of the Jesus movement.

Imagine with me, for a moment, this gathering of Jesus's apostles—those who, in John's Gospel, Jesus will call his friends—sharing all, literally *all* they've done and taught and experienced. There are stories of triumphs, yes, but also of struggle, of shortcomings, of fear. Perhaps the disciples begin as our gatherings with friends sometimes do, joking around with each other, sharing funny stories or humble-brags. And then someone, quietly at first, has the courage to speak up and share a difficult story, a story of defeat or of pain. And then another, and another. Here is the earliest community of Jesus followers gathered around a shared meal to tell stories—stories about all they were doing, experiencing, succeeding at, failing at. If this isn't church, I don't know what is. (And it should be noted that this verse is immediately followed by the story of a big free dinner.)

What would it mean for faith in college to look a lot like this early gathering of Jesus followers, sharing stories of the good and bad of our lives together, learning together in conversation with each other?

I like to start here in talking about mental health in college because in its seeming simplicity this vision of church-as-story-sharing-space gets at the "thing behind the thing": college can be tough, and inadvertently, faith communities have often communicated to young people that they aren't supposed to talk about tough things. I've lost track of how many students have told me some version of "I wasn't sure we could talk about this here." So it's powerful to say: "Yes, we can talk about that. And in talking about that with each other, we can discover ourselves, and each other, as loved: loved and accepted by each other, and loved and accepted by God." If we can facilitate this kind of story-sharing space, we are well on our way to breaking the silence and challenging the stigma which prevents many people with mental health struggles from seeking the help they need.[3]

---

3. Of course, there are other barriers to people getting the help they need, like economic inequality and a broken mental healthcare system. If you are passionate about challenging those barriers, you might check out my second book, *Grace Is a Pre-existing Condition: Faith, Systems, and Mental Healthcare*, in which I try to tackle some of these important issues.

It doesn't really take an expert to create a community of story-sharing. It does take some understanding of what makes a space safe for stories to be shared. It takes a willingness to learn; to be a model and to respect other people's vulnerabilities. It often takes someone who is willing to "go first." And it takes some healthy boundaries and balance between sharing and maintaining healthy privacy; between being in it together and also being our own unique selves. It takes, in other words, a lot of the same things that it takes to be a good friend.

You Can Be a (Good) Friend

In my ministry as a college chaplain, it's often the case that I hear about a student struggling with mental health not because they come to talk to me about it, but because a friend or a roommate does. Many times, this happens close to the end of the semester or the academic year, when things are getting stressful for everyone and a student who has been supporting a friend realizes they're not sure whether they can keep it up. They often have questions about how they can help their friend. And I often tell them that sometimes, the best thing you can do to help is to realize that you can't do it all on your own—that's why you have college chaplains, campus ministers, school counseling centers, coaches, RAs, and other kinds of services designed to support students.

We've often learned two wrong lessons when it comes to mental health and mental health struggles, and these two lessons reinforce and exacerbate each other. Wrong lesson number one, for those struggling and those who are trying to help: *I'm supposed to be able to handle things on my own.* Wrong lesson number two is: *I'm not supposed to talk about this.* So a person who is having a hard time confides in one other person—a roommate or best friend—and swears that person to secrecy. Both think the goal is to try to get through this tough thing without asking for help or talking to anyone else about it.

Don't hear me saying you shouldn't be a friend to those who are having a hard time. Being a good friend is a holy and sacred responsibility. In fact, in John's Gospel, Jesus calls the disciples his friends (John 15:15).

We're not supposed to be able to handle things all on our own—including friendship. And we can find safe and courageous spaces to talk about tough things. It takes all of us to take care of all of us. So part of what it means to be a good friend, especially to someone who is going through a difficult time with their mental health, is to know what your own limits and boundaries are, and to help expand the circle of care around your friend so that they are not isolated in their struggle. Sometimes, that might mean saying, "I care about you so much, and I'm really worried about you. I don't really know if I'm able to give you the help and support you need. Can we talk to someone else together about this?"[4] It might mean walking with your friend to talk to a chaplain or a counselor, so that they don't have to do that difficult task alone. It might mean someone in your on-campus community "going first," sharing a tough story so that others know it's ok to reach out and ask for help. Often, being a good friend means that we learn to show up and listen, that we don't necessarily have the power to fix or change things for other people.

The point is, we can't do this on our own. I'll say it again: it takes all of us to take care of all of us. That oft-quoted idea that God doesn't give a person more than they can handle? That's just not true. For one thing, that's not actually what the verse in 1 Corinthians 10:13 says, or is about—Paul is writing to the Corinthian church to warn them about idol worship, and he's not talking about suffering in this passage. For another, Paul's letters to the Corinthians are written to whole communities—communities that are meant to share in each other's burdens and help each other through difficult times. And for a third thing, Bible verses should never be used as weapons against people who are hurting, as if the point of scripture is to kick people while they're down. Our faith is designed to mutually lift us up, a point made exactly by Paul in a dif-

---

4. Helping a friend who is going through a tough time sometimes means awkward conversations, and being able to ask really direct questions about difficult topics like suicide. Contrary to popular belief, asking someone whether they have thought about suicide won't plant the idea in their head or increase the chances they'll be hurt or die by suicide; in fact, it increases the chances they'll seek help. Mental Health First Aid training is a great way to learn how to do this kind of thing well: www.mentalhealthfirstaid.org.

ferent letter to the Corinthian church, when he writes of God as the one who "consoles us in all our affliction, so that we may be able to console those who are in any affliction with the consolation with which we ourselves are consoled by God" (2 Cor. 1:4). Paul puts this statement about God specifically in the context of his own sufferings which, he writes, have sometimes been more than he can handle on his own:

> We do not want you to be unaware, brothers and sisters, of the affliction we experienced in Asia; for we were so utterly, unbearably crushed that we despaired of life itself. Indeed, we felt that we had received the sentence of death so that we would rely not on ourselves but on God who raises the dead. He who rescued us from so deadly a peril will continue to rescue us; on him we have set our hope that he will rescue us again, as you also join in helping us by your prayers, so that many will give thanks on our behalf for the blessing granted us through the prayers of many. (2 Cor. 1:8-11)

Paul, in other words, recounts a time when he was suffering so much that he wondered whether life was even worth it; and while he thanks God for his rescue from that time, he also makes sure to share that the support and love of the community of faith was a necessary component of his survival. In referencing the prayers of the church here, I am not meaning to insinuate that mental health struggles can simply be prayed away, as if challenges and suffering is the result of lack of faith.[5] Prayer, in this passage, is a sharing in the consolation offered by God to those who are afflicted. It's an intentional extension of compassion, a mindful opening of the community's heart to the one who is hurting. Paul's problems aren't fixed by prayer; rather, in the midst of his suffering he is upheld by the prayers of the community. Paul couldn't get through his time of affliction alone. Neither can any of us. You are not alone in this.

---

5. This idea, that mental illness or emotional distress is a result of lack of faith, is often taught by churches, along with beliefs that mental illness is caused by demons. I talk about, and challenge, these ideas in more depth in my first book, *Christ on the Psych Ward* (New York: Church Publishing, 2018).

You Are Not Alone

Earlier in this chapter I wrote that by stumbling into honest storytelling with each other, we can find not only shared stories of challenges but also stories of healing and hope. This is true in part because communities of faith can facilitate and reinforce the sort of activities and responses that experts recommend in responding to the college mental health crisis. For example, modern techniques of mindfulness, often taught as recognition and coping skills for people such as myself who have had to learn to live with oversized emotions, have their basis in the deep wisdom of spiritual practices passed down by faith communities throughout the centuries. Supportive connections with a community of friends help reduce the isolation that can often cause, and be the effect of, mental health challenges. A supportive community can help its members identify early on signs of distress or unhealth, and promote healthy activities. And by challenging the narrative that each person is in it alone, communities of faith on college campuses can help students get past the stigma, shame, and fear that may be associated with having to ask for help.[6]

It's more than a set of behaviors or techniques, however. It's also true that we can stumble into stories of healing and hope together because the simple act of sharing our stories with each other creates the conditions for a deep solidarity. Exactly the sort of solidarity that God expresses with humanity in the person of Jesus. Exactly the sort of solidarity that the church is meant to express with the hurts and hopes of God's world.

Imagine with me, again, those early disciples gathered around a fire with Jesus, telling stories of success and failure, doubt and conviction—stories of faith. Jesus, according to Mark's Gospel, invites the disciples

---

6. For an example of suggested types of steps colleges and universities can take to improve student mental health that I think are compatible with what I'm saying here, see Nancy Roy, "The Rise of Mental Health on College Campuses: Protecting the Emotional Health of Our Nation's College Students," *Higher Education Today*, December 17, 2018, www.higheredtoday.org/2018/12/17/rise-mental-health-college-campuses-protecting-emotional-health-nations-college-students/.

to come away with him, to rest and to have a meal together. But this sharing of stories, and this retreat from the busy-ness and stress of their lives does not lead the disciples to separate themselves from the world. Rather, it creates an opportunity for yet another radical form of ministry and welcome, as Jesus shows the disciples how there is plenty of food, rest, and community to go around. A gathering of friends for an honest accounting of life and ministry together becomes an opportunity to show God's love to the world.

That's the kind of faith community I believe can exist on college campuses: communities organized around God's radical solidarity with the world in the humanity of Jesus, communities that can celebrate with each other and mourn with each other and have honest conversations about it all, and communities that then go out into a world to learn, to grow, to feed, to serve. That's the kind of community I try to facilitate as a college chaplain and a campus minister, sometimes by "going first" with my own story of mental health struggle in order to create space for others to share, other times by sitting back and shutting up and listening to the stories and questions and explorations of students. And when I mess up, the very act of sharing honestly about those mess-ups and mishaps becomes, in turn, another instance of stumbling into story together. So if you're going to college, look for this kind of community; and if you're there already, help others find it. And if it doesn't exist, help create it. And if you're not sure you know how to do that, reach out for help—from a campus minister, chaplain, or one of the authors in this collection. Because you don't have to do this on your own. Whether "this" is finding a community, or whether "this" is facing a day or a week or a year that right now seems hopeless or scary, remember:

You are not alone.
You are not alone.
You are not alone.

Here are some resources for not being alone:

- If you or someone you know is in a crisis, you can call the National Suicide Prevention Lifeline: 1-800-273-8255. The Lifeline now also has an online chat option: https://suicidepreventionlifeline.org/chat/.

- Active Minds organizes mental health advocacy groups on many college campuses: www.activeminds.org/.

- JED Campus works with colleges and universities to improve suicide prevention efforts, substance abuse education, and student mental health: www.jedcampus.org/.

- CXMH is a podcast at the intersection of faith and mental health. It's hosted by Robert Vore, a mental health professional who previously worked as a campus minister, and Dr. Holly Oxhandler, a professor of social work at Baylor University: https://cxmhpodcast.com/.

- Mental Health First Aid USA trains people all over the country as first responders to mental health and substance abuse crises: www.mentalhealthfirstaid.org/.

- You can find more resources on mental health and faith on David's website: www.christonthepsychward.com/resources.

- Check out your denomination's webpage for resources on both mental health and campus ministry.

CHAPTER 10

HOLY SH*T

Becky Zartman

This chapter is about some of the more common terrible things that can happen to you in college. And there are many terrible things that can happen in college. I know, because I've walked with students through many of them. Most of my work as a college chaplain was telling students that they were going to be okay. But sometimes, I couldn't tell them that, because I didn't know if they were going to be okay. The most I could do was sit there with them and say, "I'm sorry. That's really shitty." And when the time was right, usually not right then, we would have a conversation about compost.

You see, I have the world's most boring hobby. I compost. I find composting utterly magical. I have a compost pile. I have compost tumblers. I keep thousands of worms in my laundry room. I don't care that it sometimes smells bad (although most compost has a delightful, loamy, earthy smell) and I don't care that some people find worms revolting. I love composting because what was dead and discarded, sometimes literally shit, is changed into that which gives life. Compost is resurrection in a box, and I am obsessed with it.

This is what I would tell students: I believe with every fiber of my soul that God does not cause bad things to happen to people so that someone else can "learn a lesson" or find Jesus. Natural disasters don't happen "for a reason," they just happen. God does not give children cancer so that their parents discover a deeper faith. That sort of thinking makes God into a sadist and nothing I know about God, not from scripture nor from my own experience, points to a God like that. Rather, in our world evil exists and we inflict suffering on each other; bodies are not perfect, and they break down. In other words, shit happens. But our God takes garbage and makes compost. God is working, even right now, to redeem all things. Even though you can't see it or even imagine it. Redemption is happening; death is being turned into life.

Do you understand the difference? This is really important. God doesn't cause suffering. But God redeems suffering and changes it into something worthwhile. This is the entire story of creation and the story of Jesus. As Christians, we believe God came here as a human and lived with us as Jesus. Jesus knows what it's like to be a young adult, to have family problems,[1] an identity crisis,[2] and what it is to suffer.[3] And then by raising Jesus from the dead, God changed death into life. God knows suffering and death intimately, and yet God is redemption and resurrection.

To be Christian is to live in the hope of resurrection. Not just our own bodily resurrection after death, but for everyday resurrection. We live in the hope that God can take the suffering and death along our way and turn it into life for us, and life for others. This is why we say in the Episcopal funeral rite, "All of us go down to the dust; yet even at the grave we make our song: Alleluia, alleluia, alleluia."[4] We don't deny the power of death. But we know that death doesn't win.

Anything can happen in college. But no matter what happens to you in the next few years, or ever, God is right there with you. Even when you are hurting so much all you can feel is a void, even when you can't imagine the sun rising again, God will never abandon you. God made you. God loves you. God longs for you to be whole. You are God's beloved child. And God will consecrate and compost these experiences into that which gives life for you and others: they will be holy shit.

You Are Never Alone

Just because you go to college doesn't mean that life doesn't stop happening. In fact, it usually feels like life goes into hyperdrive. When you're

---

1. Mark 3:31–35.
2. Luke 4:1–13.
3. Luke 22:39–46.
4. The Book of Common Prayer, 499.

away from your family for the first time, you might get enough distance to realize that your family isn't emotionally healthy. Far, far too many sexual assaults happen on campus. Mental health issues tend to percolate in the undergrad years, and easy access to drugs or alcohol fuels substance abuse. There are messy breakups. Identity crises. Money problems. Parents develop serious health concerns, people you love may die. There are car accidents. Suicides. And as a young adult, you are figuring out how to navigate these issues for the first time.

I'm not saying that college can't be a fantastic, life-giving experience, because it can. College is a fun adventure, filled with learning and discovery. But for some, the university-level coursework turns out to be the easy part, compared to the messiness of life. Sometimes the structure of classes and writing papers and taking tests is something to hold on to in the midst of chaos. This was very true for me. I had two grandfathers pass away during college, my young cousins came to live with my family, I had a massive reckoning of faith, a brutal bout with depression, and two messy breakups. Mostly, I felt like I inhabited a continual flux of identity. Who was I, anyway? And why was I here? And why didn't I fit in?

What I learned as I walked through it all was that no matter how alone I may have felt, I was never actually alone, and that I didn't need to figure it out alone. I found that I had friends and trusted adults along the way who could help me, and even more than that, wanted to help me. There were kind professors and priests and RAs and TAs and counselors and intern supervisors and adult friends from church who were all invested in helping me become myself. Somehow, all of these people came into my life when I most needed them. In the middle of the desert, when all I could feel was desolation and thirst, when I felt as though I couldn't possibly take another step, God provided me with the water that I needed to keep going.

God will provide water for you too. All along your way there will be people who are there to help you through, to love you into being. There are so many people in your institution and wider community who want to make sure you thrive in college: your chaplain, your academic advisor, your professors, your RAs, your friends. But no one is a mind reader. If you don't ask for help, they might not know that you need it. They need to be aware of your situation before they can help you, so talk to them. Let them know that you need guidance or support. Sometimes simply talking about an issue brings the issue into perspective and helps you find a way forward.

This is just how prayer works. Bring God into the workings of your daily life, because God also wants you to thrive. I'm not much for silent prayer, but in college I discovered the power of journaling. I would talk to God by writing about my life, asking God questions, or asking God for strength and clarity. Journaling helped me pay attention to how God was working, and who God was calling me to be, even in the chaos. Find a prayer practice that works for you, and stick with it. Prayer can be anything you need it to be: going for a run, doing laundry, making art, creating a quiet space in your day. Whatever it is, keep doing it, as prayer strengthens your relationship with God and helps you know in your soul that no matter what you're going through, God will be with you, and you are loved.

The Compost

College was rough for me. I'm still kind of surprised I made it through, but with grace and love, I did. What I discovered after I became a college chaplain was that God composted all of that garbage into good soil, compost for bearing good and meaningful fruit. I could speak honestly with students and tell them that they were going to get through that breakup or through that rocky transition after study abroad, that they would find a way forward into the postcollege future, that they too could find out who God made them to be. I could tell students that no matter what, God would be with them, and know from experience that what I told them was true.

The rest of this chapter is the compost of my life and ministry: terrible experiences that have been transformed into grace for myself and those I serve. Some of these experiences are explicitly spiritual, others not so much. We're going to talk about: death and existential pain (fun, right?); what you should know about how friendships change in college; and then a little bit of everything else from campus life. This chapter is written to be read straight through, or to be used as a reference when life hits the fan. Just flip to the section you need.

And before we start, one other thing: what I've written is based on my own experience in college, and the experiences of students I've had the privilege of serving as their chaplain. Know that what I offer I've found to be true for me, but not everything may ring true for you. That's alright. We're all doing the best we can as we go along, and we depend on God for the rest.

Life after Death

Nothing has the capacity to throw you into an existential crisis like someone dying that you loved very much. Dealing with the reality of death is hard, whether it's you or a friend who has experienced a loss. Supporting others, and allowing others to support you, is more important than ever.

When a Loved One Is Dying

If you have the blessing of advanced notice that a loved one is dying, do everything you can to say goodbye properly. If it is at all possible, go home. Don't worry about the tests or the papers, don't worry about your job. That stuff will work itself out later. No test is as important as saying goodbye well; besides, you're not going to perform well on that test anyway. Go home. Be with your family. Nothing is more important.

When you get there, don't be afraid of going into the room where your loved one is dying. Yes, they might look unlike themselves, and this might make you uncomfortable, but they are the person you love. Hold their hand, stroke their hair. Sing songs they sang to you when you were little. Tell them stories about all the times you've felt their love. You can say, "Do you remember that time when . . . ?" Tell them you love them, tell them what you need to tell them, tell them that you'll miss them but you'll be okay. They may be unable to respond, but know that they'll be able to hear you until the very end. Call your church and have the priest or pastor come out and pray with your family.

Sudden Death

One day it's a normal Tuesday, and then next your entire world has crumbled. Sudden loss is especially devastating, because there wasn't time to prepare emotionally and there wasn't time to say goodbye. What you can know is that the person you lost carried your love with them wherever they went during their life and they carried your love with them when they died. Nothing, not even death, can take your love for them away.

Grief

If it's at all possible, do everything in your power to get to the funeral or memorial service, especially if you were unable to be with your loved one when they died. Being present with others who are feeling this loss, praying together with those who loved your loved one truly helps, even if that is not evident in the current moment. There's also a power to the liturgy of the funeral service that helps direct you toward a healthy grieving process.

Grieving is hard work, but work that must be done. You won't know what to feel or how to feel; one minute you'll be fine, another you'll be sobbing in the closet. Eat, even when you don't feel like eating. Drag yourself outside for some fresh air. Shower. Do very basic things. Lean on your support network. Call your family. Make sure your chaplain knows what happened. Go to therapy or a grief support group.

When you come up for air, figure out what you need. Some students need to stay in school, because their work is their lifeline, and their support network is at school. Other students need to go home and support their family as they go through the beginning stages of the grieving process. When you know what you need to do, talk to your dean or advisor. They can help you navigate the process with the school, and you need to let them know what's happened.

The first year after you've lost someone will be the hardest; the earth will continue to spin and to go around the sun, even though it feels like your whole life has stopped. Birthdays, anniversaries, and holidays will continue to come, even when you're not ready for them. Stay connected with your family and friends on these hard days. Be gentle with yourself. Grieving takes time.

When a Friend Is Grieving

What do you do when a friend loses someone close to them? How are you supposed to act, what are you supposed to talk about? What can you possibly say to make it better?

Unfortunately, there is nothing you can do or say to relieve your friend of their grief. However, you can still be a good friend. Your friend will need you more than ever.

Here are some dos and don'ts:

- Don't use platitudes like, "It's all part of God's plan" or "He's in a better place."

- Do write a sympathy card that:
  - tells stories about the loved one, like, "I remember how your dad insisted on carrying your mini fridge up three flights of stairs when you moved in freshman year. He loved you so much."
  - acknowledges the depth of loss, like "I know how much [this person] means to you, and how much you valued your relationship with them. I'm so sorry to hear about your loss. I would be so happy to talk about [that person] with you whenever you're ready."

- Don't say, "Let me know how I can be helpful!" but do say "Here are my notes from the class you missed, I made a copy for you" or "I'm doing some laundry, can I throw yours in with mine?"

- Do make sure your friend is eating and gets out of their room.

- Don't be bullied by the fear of the awkward into avoiding your friend. Death is awkward. Show up anyway.

- Do keep inviting your friend along so he knows he's included.

- Do encourage your friend to let her academic dean know about her situation, and to find a chaplain or therapist who can help.

Pay for It Now, or Pay for It Later, with Interest

Some things that cause pain in life are small, the equivalent of scraping your knee. You dust yourself off, get up, and keep going. Other sources of pain, however, are more existential. What I mean by an existential pain is the kind of pain that doesn't go away if you just cover it up and pretend like it's not there. This pain could be from your family of origin: emotional, verbal, or physical abuse from a parent or relative; a culture of substance abuse; or untreated mental illness. This pain could be from some kind of trauma that you've experienced, like sexual assault, a car accident, or a loss of a loved one. This could be the pain of denying who you really are, choosing your family's choice of profession instead of yours, or denying your sexuality or gender. Pain like this can fester for years, and if this pain is ignored or covered up, it will cause major heartache and may manifest as depression, anxiety, or other mental illnesses.

What you need to know, more than anything else, is that when left unaddressed, this sort of pain doesn't go away. You can pretend to be someone else—for a while. You can dull the pain—for a while. But eventually the pain catches up to you.[5] When I would talk with students about these kinds of issues, I would tell them this: you can pay for it now or you can pay for it later, with interest. You can either work through your issues now, in your early twenties, or wait until it comes crashing down as a midlife crisis, when you have a mortgage and kids and you just wish you had those twenty years of your life back. Yes, dealing with the source of your pain is going to hurt. Actually, it's going to hurt a lot, and you may have to make some hard decisions. But you can't run away forever. Better to face your demons than let them own you, your life, and your choices.

Now, or the near future,[6] is the time for you to wrestle with those demons. If you let them stay with you, your growth as a person will be

---

5. This is what the LGBTQ+ community means when they say, "Closets kill."

6. The stress of finals may finally help you realize you need therapy; however, generally finals are not the time to start therapy. If you are safe, it's fine to wait the two weeks until finals are over.

stunted. But when you face the demons head on, and make the necessary changes, you can be free of them. Here's the thing to remember: God already knows everything there is to know about you, God has counted every hair on your head, God knows what has happened to you, God knows that for which you long. And God loves you beyond all imagining anyway and yearns for you to be made whole. God can transform the pain into a source of strength. You've made it this far, you can become your true beloved self.

When you're ready to clean house and deal with your pain, enlist some help. This process is far easier with good support. Talk to your chaplain. Go to the counseling center and find a therapist you trust.[7] Practice vulnerability by opening up to your friends and you'd be surprised to find how many of your friends have been dealing with some of the same issues. This work will be exhausting, and it won't be easy. But it's so, so worth it. Your investment will pay dividends, and your future self will thank you.

Suicide

First of all, if you are feeling suicidal, you need to put down this book and get help now. You can call the National Suicide Prevention Hotline (1-800-273-8255) and talk to someone who can help. Secondly, we don't believe that God makes mistakes when God creates people, and you have been created to be a beloved child of God, living with purpose and joy in the world. You are not a mistake. You are loved. Your presence makes the world a richer and fuller place.

College can be an especially dangerous time for people dealing with suicidal urges. It's easy to fall through the cracks in a new or impersonal system. And sometimes university administration legally can't tell par-

---

7. And find one that matches your own needs. There are therapists who specialize in different types of therapy or different issues; and it's important to find a therapist you can actually trust and with whom you can be open. If you're not able to tell your therapist the truth, the therapy doesn't work. It's okay to go to a session or two and decide it's not a good fit. Try someone else. If money is an issue, talk to your counseling center on campus for free or sliding scale services. Group therapy is another good option.

ents what's happening with their kids, as most students over eighteen are considered adults. If you are worried about someone, reach out to them. Be a good friend. Tell them you care about them. Show up and check on them. And if you are really concerned, tell an adult who is trained to help in a situation like this: a dean, a chaplain, a mental health professional. And if the situation is acute, meaning you are afraid they are going to harm themselves in the immediate future, call 911. It is better to overreact and have someone be angry with you, than it is to underreact and have a dead friend. Reach out. Ask for help.

Suicide is tragic because suicide is an abdication of the possibility of future love, and a denial of the love that surrounds us always, even when we can't feel it. And that's one of the reasons it hurts so badly when a friend or loved one commits suicide. They have denied your love for them, and they can never give love again. If you've lost someone to suicide, find a support group, online or in person. Your on-campus counseling center can point you in the right direction.

Eating Disorders

Eating disorders are life-threatening illnesses that can force you to withdraw from school, mar your personal relationships, and kill you. Eating disorders tend to develop in teenagers and young adults, and risk factors include previous dieting, anxiety, and stress. And while the exact causes of eating disorders are unknown, they are believed to be triggered in part by perfectionism, low self-esteem, or toxic relationships.[8] In other words: the stress and competition of college creates the perfect environment for eating disorders.

The most distressing thing about eating disorders (other than, you know, watching someone you care for waste away in front of your eyes) is that eating disorders distort an individual's ability to see what is true and good. What is true is that food is fuel for a healthy body; God made all bodies, and all bodies are loved by God, exactly as they are. Eating

---

8. "Eating Disorders," Mayo Clinic, February 22, 2018, www.mayoclinic.org/diseases -conditions/eating-disorders.

disorders make accurate self-perception and self-love all but impossible. That is not what God hopes for us; eating disorders mask our own belovedness with tragic consequences.

If you think you might be experiencing an eating disorder, get help now. Talk with your doctor or go to the counseling center. The sooner you get help managing your disorder, the more likely you are to return to fullness of health in body and mind. The longer a disorder goes untreated, the more dangerous it is. You are loved, as you are, and no matter what you believe right now, you deserve health and wholeness. Find someone who can help.

If you believe a friend might be experiencing an eating disorder, contact your counseling center for more information and ways to support your friend. Bring in professional help, because this is a difficult conversation that will need to be handled with care. Your chaplain will know what's possible within your university setting.

Sexual Assault

If you have been sexually assaulted, you need to know that what happened to you was *not your fault*. Nothing you were wearing, nothing you were doing made it acceptable for your attacker to harm you. What you need to do now is get help. Call someone you trust to come and be with you; you can call 1-800-656-4673, which is the sexual assault hotline for RAINN, which can direct you to a medical facility that will properly care for you, and if you choose, can conduct a sexual assault forensic exam. Call the hotline and talk with someone who can explain what all of that means (you can also find more information at www.rainn.org). No one will force you to have this exam, but if you think you even might want to pursue some semblance of justice in the future, this will help your case.

The reason sexual assault is so pernicious is that a sexual assault isn't just about what happens to a body, but is an emotional, spiritual, and psychological violation of a person's self. Because of that, it's important for a sexual assault survivor to work toward wholeness in all of these areas. This means finding help. No one wants you to walk this journey alone. Talk to your doctor, but also talk to your chaplain, they can help you find the resources you need. They will believe you and not judge you for what's happened. Your chaplain can remind you that God still loves you as much as God ever has, and that there will be a resurrection story for you. Healing takes time. But you can be whole again.

Controlled Substance Abuse

I'm going to assume that you know the reasons not to do drugs: the legal ramifications, the brain damage, risk of addiction, fueling the underground drug market that funds organized crime and human trafficking, and death by overdose.[9] You might never be tempted to do drugs recreationally, but there is another type of controlled substance on campuses which might be more tempting for the overachievers among us: Adderall and Ritalin. Often prescribed for students with legitimate learning disabilities like ADHD, there is a temptation to misuse these drugs because they have the reputation of helping you focus. But if you don't have ADHD, they aren't likely to really help. (Really, there are medical studies, go read them). There's a host of side effects, ranging from the unpleasant, like anxiety and insomnia, to the terrifying, like suicidal thoughts and cardiac arrest. If you need help focusing, try getting eight hours of sleep or a cup of coffee. But more than that, you are good enough as you are. No matter how well or how poorly you do in school, you are still beloved.

Burnout

At the Name Brand University I served, there was an odd tradition. Students wouldn't step on the university seal found in the portico of the main university building as they believed, were they to do so, that they would not graduate on time.

Most superstitions are a reflection of some deep and true fear, even if the fear manifests in silly ways. The true fear here is that there is a high

---

9. You've probably also figured out that despite the alarming abstinence messaging you may have received in high school, not all drugs are equally dangerous, and not all drugs are going to kill you instantaneously. However, the risks of permanent and irreversible harm are real. For the sake of yourself and others, be educated. However, know that no amount of education can mitigate the fact that you are tampering with your brain with chemicals from unknown sources and your actions may have an impact on other people.

percentage of students who simply do not graduate on time because of one reason or another; many students disappear for a semester or a year, and then just pop up again. There are many reasons a student may not graduate on time, but burnout is often a factor. In the great pressure cooker of college, these students were overdone.

Burnout in college happens when students have way too many obligations or try to be all things to all people. Yes, it seems like a good idea to take five courses and have an internship, a job, *and* be in extracurricular leadership while maintaining a healthy relationship with your friends and family. But everyone has limits. If you find yourself binge watching television because you can't deal with the stress; if you find yourself partying too hard each weekend just to relax; if you're having problems sleeping; if you just can't make yourself care, you might be experiencing burnout.[10]

Thanks to our roots in Judaism, Christianity has a built-in defense against burnout, if only we would participate. That defense is the spiritual practice of *sabbath*, the idea of taking a break, once a week for a whole day, and remembering that your worth is not found in what you do or what you produce, but rather your worth is found in the fact of your existence. Six days a week we *do*; one day a week, we *are*.

A sabbath need not be a Sunday: it could be a Saturday, or another day of the week you don't have class. If you can't possibly imagine spending a whole day not compulsively working on something, start with four hours and build up to a whole day. You'll find that getting rest helps keep you balanced and healthy. Even God rested on the seventh day. You can too.

Failing a Class and/or Academic Probation

Believe it or not, realizing that you are going to fail a class is an opportunity to learn something about yourself. Because when you are failing, you have to admit that something's not working. Find someone with

---

10. You may also be experiencing depression or anxiety. If you're not clear about whether or not this is the case, please see your counseling center and talk to a professional.

whom you can be totally honest (your chaplain is a great option[11]) and schedule a time to talk. What is really going on here? Do you have too much on your plate with family, friends, extracurriculars, other classes? Are you having problems paying attention or are there other complicating mental health factors? Is this just a terrible subject for you? Can you retake this class a different semester when you might not have as much going on? Is this professor purposely trying to deter students from majoring in this subject? These are just a few options; try to figure out what's actually going on. Be honest with yourself. You can't make good decisions about how to move forward without good information.

If this is a class you need to take for a major, you may need to do some real soul searching and careful discernment. For instance, you might just be terrible at physics; you need physics for the MCATs. But once you get into med school, physics doesn't really factor into what you'll be doing every day, so maybe you just need to try again, take the class to pass and get through the standardized testing, knowing that vectors aren't going to be part of your everyday professional life. But if you're trying to get to med school and microbiology is killing you, this is a time for more careful thought.

Once you've figured out what's going on, it's time to make a plan. It might be time to double-down on studying and quit playing ultimate frisbee, or it might be time to drop the class. It might be the moment to realize you'll never be a marine biologist if you truly hate biology, or it might be the time to realize that 8:00 a.m. classes are just not going to work for you unless you change your lifestyle. Whatever it is, knowing the truth is better than not knowing the truth. If you've never dropped a class before, this might be hard. But you'll be making the best choice for you. The world won't burn down. You can try again. Or not.

When it comes to being placed on academic probation, it's really time to figure out what's really going on. Discern hard and carefully,

---

11. No seriously, your chaplain is a great option. Unlike almost every other adult in the university system, your chaplain is not there to evaluate you, only to listen, support, and help you along the way. We hope you will pass your biology lab because we want you to be happy and healthy, but whether you do or not has no bearing on our relationship with you.

because the choices you make matter. Dig deep and be honest with yourself. Bring in trusted adults to the conversation. What kind of help do you need? Is this the right major for you? Is this the right school for you? What would it take to turn your college experience around? Do you need a semester (or even a year) off? Remember, no matter what you decide, you are loved. Do what you need to do to move forward.

Breaking Up

Most, but not all, students date in college. And most, but not all, of those relationships are going to end with a breakup. Generally, unless done mutually and amicably, break-ups are horrible for both the breaker and the broken.

That being said, there are opportunities to grow and learn, even in the midst of the drama and pain. Breaking up is an opportunity for honesty about yourself and the person you were with, an opportunity to acknowledge what you need in a relationship. These conversations are an opportunity to hear deep truths about oneself. Unfortunately, learning these truths are about as pleasant as listening to a recording of your own voice. That feeling of, "Ugh, is that what I sound like?" can be overpowering, but if you stick with it, you can gain some hard-earned wisdom.

But you need to be willing to have these hard conversations in order to gain this wisdom about yourself. So don't just ghost someone,[12] even if you've only been on a few dates. Not only are they also a beloved child of God who also deserves some kind of closure and the opportunity for growth, but you owe yourself the conversation as well. When you have practice articulating your needs in small ways, you can grow into being able to articulate your needs when they really matter.

The Friends from College Friendship Arc

There's more than possibly could be said here about making and keeping friends, but it's important to know that there's a pattern to friendship

---

12. With the caveat, of course, that you feel safe around this person. If you do not feel safe, you do not owe an explanation.

in a four-year college track. You make different kinds of friends along the way, and your relationship with your friends will change over time. Most of all though, remember friends are a gift from God. Make them and keep them well.

No Friends First Year Panic

Every September, on every college campus in America, there are first-year students wandering around in herds, looking beleaguered and lost. This is understandable; many campuses are huge, no one wants to go to the dining hall alone, and everyone is a little scared and trying to make friends. This results in groups of eight to twelve people wandering around campus like gazelles trying to avoid the lions of the Serengeti.

Generally, there are no lions. You aren't trapped in high school anymore. There aren't roving bullies to make your life miserable. What you can expect is benign neglect from your fellow collegians. In the best way possible, no one cares about you. This is freedom, freedom to be yourself. It takes a little practice, but lean into this freedom and try out new ways of being.

If you are a first-year student, I promise you that you will eventually make friends. You will probably even make lifelong friends, friends who will be in your wedding, friends who will be there when your first child is born, friends who will show up to your retirement party. (You may even find your spouse, who had better show up for all of these things.) But making these friends takes time. Yes, you can hang out with the people on your freshman floor, but it is important to make other friends too. Take advantage of that newfound freedom. Talk to people in class. Invite others to study sessions. Join clubs that interest you, and if no clubs interest you, start one. Be friendly, invite people to sit with you. Go to church! Focus on quality of friends, not quantity. If you try and be your own weird self, you will make a few good friends, and lots of fun friends.

The Great Friend Shakeout of Sophomore Year

There will be a huge shift in your friend experience between your first and sophomore years. When you don't live on that tight-knit first-year floor anymore, you'll discover that your real friends are the people you go out of your way to see. You'll get to know people in your major who have similar interests and personalities. Some people will float out of your social group, and that's a natural part of college. Let them go. Starting at sophomore year, most friends will be friends by choice, not by accident. This gives you freedom and time to invest in the relationships that are important to you, and is one of the reasons your sophomore and junior years can be so fun.

The Real Senioritis

At some point or another during senior year, you'll realize that your time on campus is limited. The tricky part is that different people arrive at this realization at different times, and different people react to this realization in different ways.

Usually, there are two different reactions to leaving, and each reaction, when taken to an extreme, turns into a trap. Some of your friends will want to do everything together, to savor as much of the time as possible. This is a good impulse, but taken to the extreme, everything turns into the "our last" whatever and there will be an excessive amount of nostalgia for a reality that is not yet in the past. This is exhausting. Other friends will get prickly, picking fights so they can generate the anger needed to be able to leave, and friend groups (or worse, roommates) devolve into incessant and sometimes vicious conflict.

Senior year is already stressful enough. You'll be looking for a job or applying to service years or grad school, and probably working on some kind of massive senior-year capstone project. First of all, try not to fall into either of the traps yourself. Be a good friend yourself, be kind and supportive. But when your friends go haywire, spend time with the people who are life-giving to you, and who support you. This is a really great time to lean into your church community. Soon, your whole life will hit another reset point and the relationship you have with your college friends will change. Like the sophomore year shake out, you'll keep the ones who mean the most to you, and the others will fade away. If that process starts a little early, that's okay.

Everything Else

Thankfully not everything in your life at college is going to be an earth-shattering crisis. But here are a few hard-won snippets of wisdom that have been gathered over the years.

Homesickness

If you're homesick, don't sit in your dorm room texting with your high school friends. Stay as busy as possible, make new friends, and one day you'll wake up and realize that your idea of home is more portable than you thought it was.

Money

Privilege is a real thing. Some students will have their tuition paid in cash by family members and be given a generous allowance. Other students will be barely scraping by while working two jobs and sending money home to their family while taking out loans to finance their own education. Most students will fall somewhere in between.

If you are one of those students for whom money isn't an issue, please don't assume that this is the same for your friends. Going shopping or eating out isn't just stressful, it's not even really an option. They can't take weekend trips or buy a new phone when theirs breaks. Be aware of what might be really going on as they may be unwilling to tell you. Suggest free or almost-free activities.

If you are one of the students who is barely making it, please make sure that your institution and your priest/pastor knows about your situation. Some institutions may be able to help with scholarships; local clergy can leverage connections and resources within their congregations. And hang in there. Getting an education and leveraging the social opportunities college provides can help break the cycle you find yourself in.

If you are like most students and somewhere in between these two extremities, don't try to keep up with your wealthy classmates, even though it's tempting. Live simply, like the student that you are. Avoid credit card debt at all costs, it can and will ruin your life. Leverage all of the services that your college provides while you are in college. If you want to go shopping, go to the thrift store, it's better for the environment anyway. Besides, you're young, you look great in everything. Ride a bike. Use the library. Learn how to cook. Go to a real grocery store for your food. Eat less meat. Frozen vegetables are your friend. Most importantly, make your own fun. You don't need to pay anyone to be entertained, you are smart and creative, and you probably have more time than you think you do. What you'll remember and cherish about your time at college isn't what you bought or the takeout you ate, it's the experiences that you and your friends created together. Joy is a gift from God, there's no price tag on it.

Staying Healthy

College, especially your first year, is really hard on your health. You are packed into a dorm like a sardine, you are sharing food and drinks, and you're being exposed to new and wonderful viruses your body has never experienced before. Add in some stress, a poor diet, and not getting enough sleep or exercise, and it's not a question of if you'll get sick, it's when. College students are as bad as preschoolers when it comes to communicable diseases. And preschoolers are basically walking Petri dishes, so good luck.

The key is balance. This will take a while to learn, but getting enough rest is more important than you could possibly know. Putting good food in your body and drinking lots of water is also important, as is exercise and fresh air. And for the love of all that is holy, wash your hands well and frequently. But you know all of this already. The question is, will you choose to do it? No one can do it for you, it's up to you.

If you get sick, go to the doctor. Do the things that the doctor tells you to do. And if you're still not better, go back to the doctor for a follow-up. Call the receptionist at the student health center, they can help you make an appointment. And if you're really sick, go to an urgent care or the emergency room. You're the one in charge of your health now.

Study Abroad Reverse Culture Shock

If it's at all possible for your financial situation or your major, studying abroad is one of the most challenging and wonderful things you can do in college. If you can go for at least a semester, do it, preferably in a context utterly unlike your own. Study abroad is great because it pushes your boundaries, helps you see the world from a different point of view, and can even teach you a new language.

When you study abroad, travel as much as you can. Do what you'd never thought you'd do: eat local, meet new friends, take pictures, keep a journal, be spontaneous. Also drink lots of clean water, be aware of your surroundings, don't get arrested, and try not to get robbed (passport belts seem like something your overworried grandmother gives you before you go, but trust me, you want to use them. Yes, there is a story behind this. Keep extra cash in there too.)

What no one tells you is that the hardest part of studying abroad isn't the culture shock, or the homesickness, or learning a language. The hardest part is coming home feeling like a new person while the rest of your friends stayed mostly the same. You'll have grown leaps and bounds, having experienced new places and new people, but your school will still be the school it was when you left. People will ask you how study abroad was, and you'll start off answering with, "This one time, when we were climbing in Patagonia, I saw the most amazing . . ." and they'll stop listening. You'll learn to keep your answer short. "It was great!" You might not care about things you cared a lot about before, and you might have new interests. This is ok. This reintegration into your previous life is as much a part of the process as going abroad in the first place. Be gentle with yourself as you incorporate this new experience into your identity. Seek out other students who just got back from study abroad. Journal about how you've changed. Where did you see God in study abroad? What did you learn about yourself? Do your experiences change the way you think about your vocation? With time and reflection, you'll get there, step by step. By midterms of the next semester, you'll be more comfortable in the new you.

Pending Unemployment

Every fall at the Name Brand University I served, a general sense of anxiety and panic would settle over the senior class, gradually growing until it hit a fever pitch. It was consultant recruitment season. Students at the business school would be busy interviewing and negotiating with their future employers, and by November most of those students had well-paying jobs lined up (if they hadn't had them lined up by the end of their junior year, of course.)

Here's the problem: if you're not a business school major, it doesn't make sense for you to have a job in November that starts in May, and you're not likely to have a particularly well-paying job. That's not a thing. Except it feels like a thing, and then it becomes a thing, and the next thing you know the entire senior class is in a (manufactured) identity crisis. Sure, it's nice to know what you're doing when you graduate, but it's truly okay not to know in November, or even April. It's okay to be exhausted and not roll into grad school right away too. You can take a service year. You can wait tables. You can scrounge up some money and travel. You can teach English in Southeast Asia, you can work temp jobs, you can move into an intentional community. If you don't have major family commitments, now is the time to do that thing you've always wanted to do. All of the social cues you'll be feeling will tell you that there is no time, that you must be employed as soon as possible at a grown-up job, but you have more time than you think to figure your life out. You don't need a twenty-year plan right this minute.

The job scrum is especially stressful because so much of what we've been told about our self-worth is linked to our ability to make money. Our freedom as Christians lies in the fact that we know our self-worth is only based in our belovedness. We are worthy because we're God's, and nothing we do or don't do, or how much we get paid or don't get paid can change that. I know this is easier to understand intellectually than it is emotionally, but when you finally get it on a spiritual level, you're free to make choices that require bravery. This means we don't have to do something just because everyone else is doing it. God might be, and probably is, calling you to something totally different.[13]

That's not to say that living into uncertainty while you get things figured out isn't hard, because it is. Even more so because everyone you

13. Now's a great time to go read chapter 2 on discernment, if you haven't already.

know is asking you what's next after graduation. It's perfectly reasonable to say, "It's an adventure, and I can't wait to find out."

The Definition of Experience

After I graduated from college, I ended up interning at a small nonprofit that was mostly run by nuns and volunteers. One of these volunteers was a wizened old man who came in every single day, and whose main job was harassing Congress and being an informal spiritual director to interns. He had worked to integrate the University of Alabama, he had gotten into good trouble in the Jim Crow South, he had marched with Chavez, and was now in "retirement" living in an intentional community in Washington, DC. He had been arrested more times than he could count and was utterly humble. He saw the long arc of justice for what it was—long. His name was Harold, a fount of wisdom and hilarious stories.

Almost everything I took with me from that internship, I learned from Harold.

One day at this internship, I made a big mistake. Not a normal little work mistake, but a big, hurtful kind of mistake. I was so upset I was near tears, and I went back to sit down at my desk. Without even turning around from the computer, Harold said, "The thing about experience is that by definition, you don't have it until after you need it."

It took me a few seconds to figure out what he was saying, but then I understood. I wasn't stupid or unkind or worthless or abjectly unloveable as I had been telling myself. I was just young, and had made a well-meaning and earnest, yet horrible, mistake. Everyone makes these kinds of mistakes; making mistakes is the only way we learn. There aren't any shortcuts to becoming an adult; everyone will screw up big time eventually. For the first time in a long time, I cut myself some slack. I promised myself to do better next time, and instead of losing sleep and berating myself for weeks afterwards, I let it go.

When you ask adults, even older adults, to talk about the defining moments in their lives, the choices and situations that made them who they are, invariably they point to a time in their young adulthood. Why? Because it was then they earned the experience that shaped the rest of their lives. It was their first time trying or succeeding or failing or loving or truly living. The first time you lose someone you love, the first time you get a job, the first time you say "I need help" or "I can't believe I did it," you are making life up as you go along. You earn the experience that will guide you the rest of your life.

Beloved, whatever hard or shitty thing you're going through now, know that it will pass. Earning your experience isn't easy, but it's worth doing, as this is the way you grow into the person that God is calling you to become. With the support of your friends and those who love you, and the God who created you and will never abandon you, you can overcome anything life throws at you. Stay faithful, and you'll grow flowers where the dirt used to be.

Going Deeper One day during my study abroad, I was sifting through a bargain bin in a German bookstore looking for a book in English. I found *Anna Karenina* and it changed my life. Through the lens of literature, I saw myself and my family in a new way. I know you have too much to read already, but make time for good stories. Read literature and watch films; take a class on either if you can.

My other recommendation is to read the Bible. The life and breath of human experience is in those pages. Start with the Gospels and go from there to Acts. Fight with Paul, dream about God's future with John, then go back to the past and start over again with the stories of primeval history and the patriarchs and matriarchs. Don't ever let scripture off the hook: study it, interrogate it, wrestle with it until it blesses you. Scripture is not what you learned in Sunday school, and it is not for the faint of heart, but you can and will find God there. When we learn how God has acted in history, we can learn how God is acting in the present, even in our own lives.

WHAT NOW?

Jacob was left alone; and a man wrestled with him until daybreak. When the man saw that he did not prevail against Jacob, he struck him on the hip socket; and Jacob's hip was put out of joint as he wrestled with him. Then he said, "Let me go, for the day is breaking." But Jacob said, "I will not let you go, unless you bless me." So he said to him, "What is your name?" And he said, "Jacob." Then the man said, "You shall no longer be called Jacob, but Israel, for you have striven with God and with humans, and have prevailed." Then Jacob asked him, "Please tell me your name." But he said, "Why is it that you ask my name?" And there he blessed him. So Jacob called the place Peniel, saying, "For I have seen God face to face, and yet my life is preserved." (Gen. 32:24–30)

A long time ago, by a river, two people wrestled all night. One was a man named Jacob, but the other's identity was hidden. Some have said that Jacob wrestled an angel, or God incarnate, or that it was just a vision. Regardless, the story of Jacob is a lot like college. Here at the end of these pages, your journey is beginning. What now? And just as we started with an invitation, we leave you with another invitation . . . and a story.

But first, a little context for our story: Jacob was a hustler. He swindled for his birthright and deceived his father and twin brother. The deception is reciprocated though when he hopes to marry a woman named Rachel: his father-in-law, Laban, gets Jacob horribly drunk and the next morning, Jacob awakens to find he is married to Leah, Rachel's sister! ("Leah" in Hebrew means something like "cow's eyes.") Jacob eventually also marries Rachel and returns the favor by swindling his father-in-law out of his best livestock and wealth. As he's returning home with all of his family and newfound wealth (numerous wives, children, servants, and thousands of livestock), his twin brother Esau (the one from whom he stole the inheritance) gets word Jacob is coming and rallies an army.

So Jacob, ever the swindler, hedges his bet in case Esau attacks. Jacob divides his family in two groups, sends lavish gifts to his brother, and then sends his family out ahead of him to greet Esau. The plan works—Esau is moved with compassion and forgiveness when he sees his nieces and nephews and gifts. This is where our story picks up: Jacob has sent them all ahead and stays behind by himself.

It is there, on that riverbank, where Jacob moves beyond a life of deception and becomes who he really is. Jacob's destiny is forever changed as he proves himself to be tenacious and bold despite his pain. Jacob's struggle results in a new identity; from now on Jacob is Israel, which literally means, "wrestler of God." In many ways, Jacob's struggle is your struggle: the struggle of coming into one's self. At times, you will be alone. You will be wounded. And yet, as Jacob walked away from his encounter with the divine as "God-wrestler," you will walk away from your wrestling match with a blessing and a new identity: "Beloved."

You are meant to wrestle. This account leaves us with more questions than answers, and rightly so. We don't get our answers handed to us, because just as you were made to be beloved, you were also made to wrestle in your relationship with God. God says, "Let me go!" and Jacob does not let God go. Many of us arrived in college with an idea to explore other expressions of faith. Some become atheist or agnostic in this new freedom. Some, in dualistic thinking find faith irreconcilable with academia, science, suffering, and the problem of evil, and attempt to write-off God for a few years. Whatever the case may be for you, the fact that you are skeptical or questioning is very good. Rather than seeing this as a letting go of God, this is a wrestling with God until the truth and the deeper meaning of who you are is discovered. What a paradox: you've decided to let go of God only to discover that your wrestling intensifies.

Doubt and faith are two sides of the same coin, and as such, doubt is actually good. Writer Anne Lamott said: "I have a lot of faith. But I am also afraid a lot, and have no real certainty about anything. . . . I remembered something a pastor had told me—that the opposite of faith is not doubt, but certainty. Certainty is missing the point entirely. Faith includes noticing the mess, the emptiness and discomfort, and letting it be there until some light returns."[1] Doubt creates the space necessary for us to wrestle with God, and our wrestling is how we become people of mature faith and claim our own belovedness.

You are left on your own, apart from your family. You've left your family for a few years to figure out who you are and whose you are. And in some ways you really are on your own. Only you can do the struggling necessary to grow into yourself. Leaving and returning is natural, but we do not return unchanged. We are transformed by our wrestling and given a new identity. How could things ever be the same? What will happen now? Like Jacob, you may be wondering, will you be met with grace or violence? Will you be met with love and acceptance for who you are or will you find rejection and hatred? Hopefully, like the newly minted Israel, you are met with forgiveness, grace, and your own belovedness, welcomed with open arms by your sibling. Even when you're not, and more wrestling awaits, you engage with the comfort that you are beloved and no one can change it.

You are wounded. Just when it feels like you're winning or succeeding at life, your hip pops out of socket and makes you limp. Shit happens. Suffering and heartbreak wound us deeply. Even with this wound, however, we still are met with blessing. Even if it was all a dream (but who's to say that makes the encounter any less real), then the wound he receives is a loss of ego. Or perhaps our sparring partner is our own shame, loneliness, loss, or unworthiness. We, like Jacob, now must face life with a limp. We are meant to let go of who we think we are. "Ego" simply means "I," but it can become selfish or conceited in thinking and becomes our center instead of the love of Jesus. The wrestling will strip away our ego and leave behind belovedness.

You won't give up. Jacob would not give up, even though he was wounded, even though the wrestling match dragged on throughout the night and into the dawn, even though Jacob was wrestling with God. And even then, Jacob demanded a blessing from God—and got even

---

1. Anne Lamott, *Plan B: Further Thoughts on Faith* (New York: Riverhead Books, 2005), 236.

more than he asked for when he was gifted a new name in addition to a blessing. Wrestle with God as long as you need to wrestle. Some people's wrestling matches are short; some last entire lifetimes. It doesn't matter how long it takes, as long as you don't give up on the struggle of your relationship with God. Keep God close, and hang on tight. It's worth it.

You receive a new name. Jacob was struggling with who he was. He wanted to be his brother and had to deceive to get what he wanted. He's unsure if he can live into his father's blessing. So it makes sense that when his story is at its most tense moment, God shows up to remind him who he is. Just as Jacob is now "God-wrestler," your new name is "Beloved." If God is love, that is, not a proper noun but instead a verb or attribute, then your true name is also essence and relationship bound up in the divine. When you claim your true identity as Beloved, you are set free to be your truest self, a self that is free from the fear of failure, a self that discerns God's call, a self that grows and flourishes in right relationships.

You will be blessed. God blesses Israel, and in doing so keeps God's promise to Israel's grandfather, Abraham. This blessing is in turn a manifestation of the dream of the original blessing at the Garden (if you can recall back to chapter 1). Or perhaps a better example of blessing would be artist and musician, Lizzo. My friend Liz recently went to a Lizzo concert and came back glowing. She said it was the best concert experience she ever had. "Everyone, everyone, was positive and people even complimented me on my outfit!" What a glimpse of the beloved community: where everyone sees everyone else's God-given, intrinsic value. Just as body positivity at a Lizzo concert can be refreshing and infectious, so can the language of blessing. If you treasure it, you will give it away. And the more you give it away, your community will begin to transform into beloved community. Israel's blessing rested on Judah whose great-great-great-great-great grandson was Jesus. The blessing asks to be passed on. What will you do with it?

That was the story. Now here's the invitation: enter the all-out cage match with God. Wrestle with God through the pain and until the dawn. Don't let God go until God blesses you, and you claim your new identity as Beloved.

HOW TO FIND A CAMPUS MINISTRY

The first and best place to start when you are looking for a campus ministry is your campus ministry office, sometimes known as the spirituality center. Hopefully what you'll find is a healthy and collaborative group of chaplains who want to see you thrive along your spiritual journey. However, not all campuses are equipped with such a center. What then?

Here are some other ways you might find a spiritual community who can support you on your way:

- Look up your denomination's governing body (if you're Episcopal, this is a diocese; if you are Lutheran, this is a synod; if you're Presbyterian, this is a presbytery; if you're Methodist, this is an Annual Conference, etc.) and see if there are resources. You can call and ask them; they'd be happy to hear from you.

- Find churches closest to campus and inquire there. Check out their website and go on a Sunday morning. What you may discover is that the Lutherans have a robust program but the Episcopalians don't; in this case, do not hesitate to go to the local Lutheran Church. We're all playing on the same team, please don't give up on church community because the denominational lines are blurred. However, it's a good idea to ask if this church is open and affirming when it comes to the LGBTQ+ community.

- Is there absolutely nothing happening? Start your own. Gather a few like-minded friends and start a small group with this book; see where it leads you. Never underestimate the power of a few good faithful friends. If you get something started, reach out to your local church or governing body; they may be willing to provide some resources to you if the group is already up and running. You may also be able to apply for funding from your university or student government.

A Word of Caution about Parachurch Ministries

On any campus you can expect the presence of parachurch ministries, which are organizations made up of largely nondenominational churches. They will likely be aggressively present in the beginning of the school year. These groups are not necessarily bad, but they should be approached with extreme caution. If the Christian group or church is friendly and loving at first and you feel community and belonging, great. But if that belonging is contingent on a strict moral code, or relies on only one "correct" reading of scripture, it might be time to start asking questions. If the leaders or the group becomes insistent on pointing out all the ways you're sinning or not "in" until you believe something, you have a right to be skeptical. You have the right to leave if your values differ from theirs, and don't allow yourself to be harangued or guilted into returning to the group. If they continue to harass you, report them to your institution. There's a good chance they've been harassing other students as well. Most institutions of higher education allow religious groups but with limits on "proselytizing" (fancy word for trying to get "converts"). If the group is shaming you into converting, report the bias to administration.

The fact is, campuses are rampant with certain Christian voices who have come to "save souls" from damnation and from academia. We don't think academia and Christianity actually compete, and the thing about saving souls is that God has already accomplished it. The notion of "saving souls" or talking about being "winsome" is seriously not giving credit to God for the work done at Creation, the Incarnation, the Crucifixion, and above all, the Resurrection. God's love is all encompassing, and will not and cannot be denied to anyone, no matter what these groups may tell you.

Before you join a parachurch organization or even attend one of their events, ask some questions. How does this organization treat LGBTQ+ people? Are queer people welcomed as equals and can they become part of the leadership while being openly gay? Are there women in leadership? What kind of language does this organization use for God? How does this organization read scripture? Asking these questions on the front end is so important. If you feel as though these answers are evasive, they are. Walk away.

APPENDIX 2

THE *OBSERVATIO*

The *Observatio* was developed by the Reverend Stacy Alan to prepare students for the classic Ignatian spiritual exercise, the *Examen*. The *Observatio* can be journaled, or simply prayed. This is a great prayer practice for individuals in time of discernment. At the close of each day, take some time to reflect:

- When/where was I aware of God today?
- When/where did God seem absent or far away?
- What else did I notice about God and me today?

There is no "right" experience: you may go through a whole day with no awareness of God, or you may be paying attention and not perceive anything you recognize as God. The point of this practice is to learn to pay attention spiritually and to recognize the ways that God shows up *for you*. Whether you have some kind of sublime experience with angels and trumpets or something that seems just vaguely God-like, whether it is a clearly happy or peaceful feeling or something more troubling or frustrating, you can't get this wrong. One of the assumptions of this exercise is that God is always ready to show up and desires a relationship with us. If we miss God, or forgot to pay attention, God will show up again. It's not about duty or obligation, but invitation, and about building up habits and spiritual muscle memory.

Once you feel like you can recognize when God shows up for you during the day, then you could move on to the classic Ignatian prayer: *the Examen*. This is a daily review, in dialogue with God, of your day. There are many variations, but it is basically these five steps:

1. Become aware of God's presence.

2. Review the day with gratitude and honesty: When was I my best self? When was I less than my best self? When was I aware of God's presence?

3. Pay attention to your emotions.

4. Choose one feature of the day and pray from it.

5. Look toward tomorrow.

More resources on *the Examen* can be found here:
www.ignatianspirituality.com/ignatian-prayer/the-examen/

BELOVEDNESS SMALL GROUP DISCUSSION GUIDE

This small-group discussion guide is designed for seniors in high school and college students. Of course, you can just grab the book, flip to the questions, and talk about them with your friends. But if you're looking for a program for your youth group or campus ministry, or you're thinking about starting a small group on your campus, this is a great place to start.

Starting a Small Group

Identify a Facilitator

Facilitating a conversation means to ease the conversation along, which is to say the facilitator helps the conversation to happen. This means that the facilitator doesn't need to have answers to the questions. In fact, the facilitator probably shouldn't have answers to the questions. For that matter, it's best if the facilitator is not a clergyperson. Anyone who is willing to communicate with the group and who is assertive enough to keep the discussion on track could be a facilitator.

Gather the Group

While there are benefits to creating a space for conversation around certain identities (for instance, a group entirely of people who identify as women, or students of color, or LGBTQ+ students), there are also benefits of intentionally creating a group of students with different life experiences. We encourage you to think about inviting students that don't look like you, aren't from the same socioeconomic bracket, or have the same sexual orientation or gender identity.

- Make personal invitations to the group. Ask your participants to see if they would know someone else interested in participating.

- When you make your invitations, be clear about participation expectations. The best small group experiences are made in the groups that build trust over a period of time. Trust is not created by dropping in and out. Participants should plan on missing no more than two sessions.

- Eight to fourteen participants is the optimal size for a small group. Jesus was onto something: twelve is the perfect number. Any larger than fourteen, and you should split the group in two.

Figure Out Logistics

Answer the following questions:

- Where and when will the small group meet?

- Is this location safe and accessible for everyone in the group?

- Is this location available for each of the ten sessions?

- What date will the group start, and how often will you meet?

- What is the best way to reach participants if there is a last-minute change?

When the dates are set, give as much notice as possible to participants. Some ideas for on-campus meeting spaces include a library study room, a dorm common room, a nearby church, or a space in the campus chapel/religious center.

This discussion guide is designed to be used one chapter per session, which is a series of ten sessions. However, groups could choose to tackle two chapters at a time by scheduling five 90-minute sessions.

First Small Group Session (75 minutes)

The first small group session is slightly different and a bit longer than the other sessions. During the first session, the group will have to establish group norms, which accounts for the extra fifteen minutes.

Opening Prayer (5 minutes)

Check-in (15 minutes)

Group Norms (15 minutes)

Conversation (35 minutes)

Wrapping Up and Closing Prayer (5 minutes)

Opening Prayer (5 minutes)

Gather the participants around a table or in a circle of chairs, and open the session with prayer. The facilitator may choose to ask participants for prayer requests and then pray extemporaneously, or the facilitator may choose to open with this prayer found in The Book of Common Prayer:

> O God, you manifest in your servants the signs of your presence: Send forth upon us the spirit of love, that in companionship with one another your abounding grace may increase among us; through Jesus Christ our Lord. *Amen.* (BCP, 125)

Check-In (15 minutes)

Check-in is a time for the group to get to know one another and to reconnect since the last session. Check-in is different from small group discussion in which participants respond to the conversation. During check-in, each person is invited to respond to the check-in prompt. The facilitator asks the check-in question, and then invites someone to speak. That person can either answer the question or pass the question. Whether they answer or pass, that person asks the next person to answer. At the end, the facilitator should ensure that everyone who passed has another opportunity to answer. No one must answer the question, although all should be invited.

Invite the group to share their responses to the check-in question for the chapter you'll be discussing.

Establishing Group Norms (15 minutes)

Groups work best when norms are established. This means that the group should decide how the group should function. The facilitator should help the group come to a consensus on the following topics:

Confidentiality

- What may or may not be shared with others who are not in the group?
- Can you share a story with that person's permission?

Technology

- Will phones be off, on the table, or in use?

Respect

- What are expectations about punctuality?
- What are group expectations during conversation? Should group members be allowed to interrupt or talk over others?

As each norm is decided, the facilitator writes the norm down. Some groups find it easiest to use newsprint and markers, others find it perfectly fine to write the norms down and share them at a later time (as in an e-mail, or printed at the next session) so everyone has the norms for reference.

The specifics of what each group decides is less important than the fact that the group decided what's best for the group. This process provides buy-in and a reference point for acceptable and nonacceptable behavior. After the group norms have been set, the facilitator should feel empowered to reference the group's norms if a behavior is becoming a problem. For instance, if a participant keeps interrupting others, the facilitator can remind the group that the group decided that interruptions were not acceptable. If a group consistently violates norms, a facilitator can revisit the group norms, or lead the group in another discussion about norms. They may need to be amended.

Small Group Discussion (35 minutes)

The purpose of small group discussion is to grow in relationship with others and with God. These relationships are nurtured in open, creative, and life-giving conversations. Before the session, the facilitator should read and reflect on the chapter, and prepare for the discussion by reviewing the questions. Facilitators should consider which questions would resound with this particular group of people.

The facilitator should open with a discussion question, and allow participants to have a conversation. Here are some things to remember:

- Facilitators don't have to fill every awkward silence. Silence can be a fruitful experience; people may be reflecting or getting ready to say something profound.

- Sometimes a group may get "stuck" on one question, but if everyone is engaged with the topic and finding the conversation meaningful, there is no need to go through all of the questions. The goal of the conversation is reflection on the topic and relationship building; if this is happening, you're doing it right.

- It's okay to make up your own discussion questions. The ones included are only meant to give you a place to start.

- Not every person will answer every question.

- It is the facilitator's job to shepherd the conversation if one person is dominating, or if a few people are not participating. Invite those who haven't spoken to speak.

- Keep an eye on the time. It's easy to lose track when the discussion is going well.

Sometimes, the facilitator will have to ask some follow-up questions to keep the conversation going. Here are some helpful follow-up questions:

- How did that make you feel?

- Tell us more about that.

- What made you think of that?

Wrapping Up and Closing Prayer (5 minutes)

The facilitator should invite participants to take a moment and think about where God showed up in this conversation. If there is enough time, the facilitator could invite participants to share their insights.

Close with prayer, either extemporaneous, or a prayer from The Book of Common Prayer like *A General Thanksgiving* found on page 836.

Subsequent Small Group Sessions

The remaining sessions are run exactly like the first session, with the omission of the group norms conversation. These sessions should last 60 minutes.

Opening Prayer (5 minutes)

Check-in (15 minutes)

Conversation (35 minutes)

Wrapping-Up Closing Prayer (5 minutes)

Chapter/Session Discussion Questions

Chapter 1: Belovedness

Check-In Question:

- Name something that makes you *you*.

Questions for Discussion:

1. This chapter lays out the concept of "belovedness." What sorts of messages have you received from the church and world about your own belovedness?

2. What gets in the way of claiming your belovedness as truth? What are the competing voices telling you who you are?

3. In your own experience, have you found people to be inherently good or inherently evil?

4. James writes, "Jesus Christ is at the beginning, middle, and end of the story of belovedness." How has your relationship with God changed over time?

5. What would your life look like if you lived your life from a place of belovedness?

Chapter 2: Making Choices

Check-In Question:

- Share an experience of a time when life didn't go according to plan. What happened next?

Questions for Discussion:

1. How might understanding that God has plans for you, not just a plan, change your discernment?

2. How are you (or how are you not) paying attention?

3. Are you pursuing your own passions and gifts, or fulfilling expectations of your parents or peers?

4. When you think about your future, what gives you energy? What takes that energy away?

5. Stacy writes, "Perhaps discernment isn't so much about getting things 'right,' but rather about being faithful." How could this shift your perspective about discovering God's calling for you?

Chapter 3: Success and Failure

Check-In Question:

■ Talk about a time when you thought you "failed." Have you come to see this failure as a gift?

Questions for Discussion:

1. How has a rejection or failure helped you to become more resilient?

2. If you step back, like the disciples in Mark 6, to reflect upon the path that led you to where you are, what comes to mind?

3. Who in your life is a good example of someone who embodies the virtue of humility? What can you learn from their life?

4. Brandon writes, "Failure is a moment of honest examination of our lives." What truths have you discovered through your failure?

5. Where have you discovered grace in your own life?

Chapter 4: Relationships

Check-In Question:

■ To whom and to what do you belong? Where and to whom do you feel a sense of belonging?

Questions for Discussion:

1. When you were little, what did you want to be when you grew up? How has your relationship with this question (and other questions like it) changed over time?

2. Do you tend to overextend in your relationships, or do you tend to underextend? Why do you think that is so?

3. How has your relationship with your family changed since you came to college?

4. How would you approach your relationships differently if you could trust that God was holding your relationships for you?

5. How can you move from a performance-centered life to one of empathy? Who are your neighbors on campus?

Chapter 5: Worship

Check-in Question:

▨ Who in your life has been a "starter batch" for your faith?

Questions for Discussion:

1. When have you seen glimpses of God in your life? How do you respond to these?

2. What does "you cannot know yourself by yourself" mean to you?

3. How might you position yourself toward the gospel during your week?

4. What are prayer practices that you have tried that didn't work for you? What prayer practices have you tried that do work for you?

5. If you "cannot win your life," what becomes more important? What becomes less important?

Chapter 6: God Made the Rainbow

Check-In Question:

- Have you been burned by the church, religion, or terrible theology? Have you been blessed by the church, religion, or loving theology?

Questions for Discussion:

1. How has a hardship in your life helped you become a person with more integrity or grace?

2. How could your view of God or scripture change if you think of Jesus as an ally?

3. Bishop Michael Curry (now Presiding Bishop Michael Curry) asked Adrienne, "Where are you and Jesus right now?" Where are *you* and Jesus right now?

4. Where is home for you? What does it mean to follow Jesus to a new home?

5. Where can you find or create Brave Space on campus?

Chapter 7: Sex

Check-In Question:

- How did your church or parents talk to you about sex, if at all?

Questions for Discussion:

1. What is your theology of sexuality? Is this something about which you've given much thought? Why or why not?

2. How might your thinking about sex change when the conversation starts from a place of goodness instead of sinfulness?

3. God created us to be subjects, not objects, and yet we are told the lie that our worth is based on how we look or what we do. Talk about a time that you felt objectified. How can we work toward deobjectifying one another on campus and in our wider culture?

4. Samantha recommends asking two questions before engaging in intimacy: First, in this moment, is this an expression of love? Second, at this time, will this expression affirm your dignity? How would asking and answering these questions change your relationships?

5. Has your thinking about sin changed over the course of reading this chapter or book?

Chapter 8: Partying

Check-In Question:

▓ Jesus loved to celebrate and have a good time. What are your favorite ways to have fun or celebrate?

Questions for Discussion:

1. Are you surprised to hear that college students spend less time partying than previous generations? Does that seem true on your campus?

2. Talk about a time you lost your balance and fell off of the "seesaw" of partying. (Or talk about a time that someone else's actions directly affected you.) What did you learn from that experience?

3. What does "everything is permissible but not everything is beneficial" mean in your own life?

4. How might you have more balance in your college life? Where does your life feel in balance, and where does your life feel out of balance? What does an ideal party look like to you?

Chapter 9: Mental Health

Check-In Question:

▓ David writes, "It takes all of us to take care of all of us." What does that look like in your own life?

Questions for Discussion:

1. Tell a story about a time that you were brave and "went first." What happened?

2. The life of a college student is stressful for many reasons. How do you deal with stress in healthy or unhealthy ways?

3. What spaces around campus are safe spaces that allow you to practice vulnerability? What are not safe spaces?

4. Name the resources on your campus for mental health. Are they easy to access? Do students use them?

5. How does a theology of belovedness (believing that we were created by God to be loved and to love one another) change how you view mental health in yourself and your fellow students?

Chapter 10: Sh*t Happens

Check-In Question:

■ "The thing about experience is that by definition, you don't have it until after you need it." Name an experience you've earned on campus. What advice would you give to next year's freshman class?

Questions for Discussion:

1. Tell a story about a time when God composted a bad experience into something good. What fruits or flowers are now growing from that compost?

2. Who are the people in your life who can help you navigate the ups and downs of college?

3. Becky writes, "Pay for it now, or pay for it later, with interest." What issue in your life are you feeling called to work on now?

4. If the general attitude on campus is indifference instead of bullying or fear, how might you let go of inhibitions and be more fully yourself?

5. How are you practicing self-care on campus? What is one thing you could do to better care for your body, mind, or spirit?

ACKNOWLEDGMENTS

James's Acknowledgments

I am ever so grateful to all who made this book possible and to all those who encouraged me to pursue this dream. First, to my students whom I love dearly: you have been ever constant in my mind in the shaping of this book. To students I have yet to meet and never will: I hope you find yourself, deep meaning, and the love of the One who made you. Thanks, Dana, and thanks to my intern, Kenly, for your edits, suggestions, and deep conversations. Thank you to my readers: Lauren Burns, Hannah Goodwin, Lee Mendenhall, and Nick VanHorn for your affirmations and for giving your honest and compassionate feedback. To my colleagues and fellow campus ministers, especially the contributing authors: Ben Adams, Stacy Alan, Samantha Clare, David Finnegan-Hosey, Brandon Harris, Adrienne Koch, and Olivia Lane—your wealth of wisdom and beautiful words transformed this book into something beyond what I could've imagined. Thanks, Sharon Ely Pearson, our amazing editor and CPI! Thanks most of all to Becky for your ability to take an idea we drew on napkins at a conference and make it come to fruition. You are an inspiration and I am deeply blessed by your friendship.

I am ever so grateful to my wife, Samantha: my love, my steadfast (and my greatest and most trusted critic). Thank you for enduring late nights of editing my terrible grammar. Everyone else thanks you for saying "no" to my terrible puns. Thank you my darling girls, Corinne and Grace, for your unconditional love. You may one day find yourselves in college and in need of wisdom and hope that you will both find it in us as parents and perhaps from these pages as well.

Becky's Acknowledgments

Like all things in Christian life, this book project would have been impossible alone.

My first acknowledgment must be to Jason Evans, who called me one summer morning to ask if I'd like to be a college chaplain, and who has been a steadfast encourager, mentor, and friend. I'm also grateful for the Episcopal Diocese of Washington's support of campus ministry, and the gracious welcome from the Office of Campus Ministry at Georgetown University. I'm also so grateful for my clergy colleagues in Georgetown, especially the Rev. Gini Gerbasi for her friendship and love, and the Rev. Brett Davis, who with Gini took up the baton of Commonplace after we moved to Houston. And to all of my students, who accepted me for me and taught me how to be a better human and priest. I have loved watching you grow and thrive.

A huge thanks to our contributing authors for their wisdom, insight, and collegiality. You are so good at your work, and your work is so important. Most especially, I'm grateful for my partner in this endeavor, James, without whom this project would have never materialized. Thank goodness for our willingness to stick it out for the sake of the other.

Special thanks to the Very Rev. Barkley Thompson and the people of Christ Church Cathedral, Houston, who have welcomed me into a new role and city while allowing me to reflect on my past few years. Also to Molly Cooke and Ellie Singer, my second readers, and Sharon Ely Pearson, our editor at Church Publishing Incorporated.

I am especially grateful for my husband, Josh, whose love (and patience) is never failing, and for my daughter, Perpetua, who spent the first four years of her life on a college campus. You are a joy.

MEET THE CONTRIBUTORS

Ben Adams went to John Carroll University on the east side of Cleveland, Ohio, where he majored in economics and finance. He now lives in Chicago with his wife, Tara, and their dog, Gracie. If he's not at home baking sourdough, brewing kombucha, playing his ukulele, or just hanging out, then you can usually find him pastoring in and around Grace Episcopal Church in Chicago's South Loop. He gets back and forth to work primarily on his bike, but for shorter trips he prefers to skateboard. Outside of his work and at-home hobbies, he serves as an assistant coach for the University of Chicago wrestling team and builds power through community organizing with The People's Lobby.

Stacy Alan is an alumna of Seattle University. After traveling and studying Spanish in Central America, she attended Union Theological Seminary, spending a year at the Seminario Bíblico Latinamericano in San José, Costa Rica. After graduating, she worked at Holy Apostles Soup Kitchen, the largest private emergency feeding program in New York City. She was ordained in the Diocese of New York in 1998. Before coming to Chicago, Stacy served at St. Luke's Episcopal Church in Kalamazoo, Michigan. Since January 2005, Stacy has been the chaplain at Brent House, the Episcopal Center at the University of Chicago. She recently received a certificate in spiritual direction in the Ignatian Exercises. She is married to improv actor and playwright John Poole and has two adult children.

Samantha Clare serves as the Episcopal chaplain to the University of Arkansas in Fayetteville with St. Martin's Episcopal Center. She has a passion for spreading Jesus's call for social justice and making connections between daily and spiritual lives in pursuit of wholeness and authenticity. Samantha graduated from Cottey College in Nevada, Missouri, with an associate of arts degree. She transferred to the University of California, Santa Cruz, and completed a bachelor of arts in psychology. She is currently in a master of divinity program at Bexley Seabury Seminary. She blogs at samanthaclare.me.

James Franklin serves as campus and young adult missioner in Winston Salem, North Carolina, primarily at Wake Forest University. He holds degrees from Seminary of the Southwest in Austin, Texas (master of divinity) and UNC Chapel Hill (bachelor of arts). James landed his dream job in campus ministry, combining his love of coaching students, providing spiritual direction, preaching, writing, and helping create beloved community. He loves exploring the mountains of North Carolina and lives in Winston Salem with his wife and daughters.

David Finnegan-Hosey is college chaplain and director of campus ministries at Barton College, having previously served campus ministries at Georgetown University, American University, and the University of Hawai'i Manoa. He holds an MDiv from Wesley Theological Seminary in Washington, DC, and a bachelor of arts in international studies from Washington College in Chestertown, Maryland. David is also the author of *Christ on the Psych Ward* and *Grace Is a Pre-existing Condition: Faith, Systems, and Mental Healthcare*. David lives in Wilson, North Carolina, with his wife, Leigh, and their dog, Penny Lane. Follow him at davidfinneganhosey.com.

 **Brandon Harris** is a graduate of The Lincoln University of Pennsylvania (the nation's first historically black college) where he obtained a bachelor of arts in political science and religion. He attended Candler School of Theology at Emory University in Atlanta, Georgia, where he earned a master of divinity with certificates in Black Church Studies and Baptist Studies. He currently serves as the Protestant chaplain to the main campus at Georgetown University. He is ordained in the American Baptist Churches USA and the Progressive National Baptist Convention.

 **Adrienne Koch** was most recently the young adult missioner and campus minister for the Raleigh Area in the Episcopal Diocese of North Carolina and adjunct faculty at Duke University Divinity School. She received her BA in liberal arts from Malone College in 2004, with concentrations in theology, psychology, and communications, and her MDiv from Duke in 2011 with a certificate of studies in gender, theology, and ministry. She completed her Anglican coursework at Sewanee and is in the process of becoming a certified teacher of the Narrative Enneagram. Adrienne moved to Cleveland, Ohio, in the fall of 2019. She is currently a priest at Trinity Cathedral.

 **Olivia Lane** has specialized in chaplaincy and spiritual formation for the past decade. She began her career in neurosciences and psychiatric hospital chaplaincy, and most recently served as the Protestant chaplain for spiritual formation at Georgetown University. She earned her undergraduate degree with honors in music performance from The University of Tulsa, and holds a master of divinity from Princeton Theological Seminary. She is ordained in the Presbyterian Church (USA) and currently writes and ministers in the Eastern Oklahoma Presbytery.

Jonathan Melton has served as a priest for twelve years now, including as chaplain to the St. Francis House Episcopal Student Center at the University of Wisconsin-Madison from 2012 to 2019. Go Badgers! He now serves as the associate priest at Holy Trinity by the Lake in Heath, Texas, not far from where he grew up. Jonathan attended Wheaton College, earning his BA in economics, before earning his master of divinity at Duke Divinity School. He is a longtime blogger, avid reader, novice guitarist, commuter-type cyclist, and occasional knitter, married to Rebekah, with three wonderful children.

Becky Zartman grew up in Central Pennsylvania. She majored in philosophy at Gettysburg College with a minor in peace and justice studies. After college, Becky moved to Washington, DC, because all of her friends did, and it worked out surprisingly well. She graduated from Virginia Theological Seminary with an MDiv in 2013. Becky has worked as assisting clergy at St. Thomas, Dupont Circle, and as the Episcopal missioner to Georgetown University. She is currently the Canon for Welcome and Evangelism at Christ Church Cathedral, Houston.